PHOTOSHOP PROJECTS

JOHN SLATER

In easy steps is an imprint of Computer Step
Southfield Road . Southam
Warwickshire CV47 0FB . United Kingdom
www.ineasysteps.com

Notice of Liability

Every effort has been made to ensure that this book contains accurate and current information. However, Computer Step and the author shall not be liable for any loss or damage suffered by readers as a result of any information contained herein.

Trademarks

Photoshop® is a registered trademark of Adobe Systems Incorporated. All other trademarks are acknowledged as belonging to their respective companies.

Printed and bound in the United Kingdom

ISBN 1-84078-276-5

Contents

Image Correction – Basic & Creative

Perspective

Automate, Actions & Batch

12

169

Cheat at Illustration

13

179

Picture Framer

14

193

Five Minute Wonders

211

Understanding Color Management

225

Index

235

Images (in alphabetical order)

If you want to follow the examples shown in this book the images can be downloaded free of charge from the website:

www.ineasysteps.com

Alex.jpg	Alice.jpg	Auckland.jpg	Balloons.jpg	Bank.jpg
BayHotel.jpg	BigBen.jpg	BluFlowers.jpg	Boatplan.jpg	BoatplanEND.jpg
Broadway.jpg	Builder.jpg	Bus.jpg	Canary.jpg	Clouds.jpg
Clown.jpg	Digital Test.tif	Dress1.jpg	Dress2.jpg	Dress3.jpg
DSC_1183.jpg	Emerald.jpg	FashionShow.jpg	Flowers.jpg	Frame.jpg
Grayshirt.jpg	GreenPattern.jpg	Heather.jpg	Ice.jpg	Iceboat.jpg
Inthepink.jpg	Jockeys.jpg	John.jpg	LCF shoot.tif	LCFshootpres....
Liberty.psd	LibertyEND.jpg	LinePattern.tif	Lion.jpg	Liz.jpg

Images (continued)

This layout was created using the Automate command described on page 170

Quick Start

This book assumes that you have dabbled with Photoshop but have not really progressed. You know how to use a mouse but not much more. The screenshots shown are from Photoshop CS but most of the techniques apply to all versions, regardless of whether you are using a Windows or a Mac computer. This is not just a book of projects. The aim is to stimulate your creative talent. Initial chapters are very simple, but techniques become more involved and more professional as you progress. You will metamorphose from a raw beginner to a good, intermediate standard. Enjoy and have fun!

Covers

Images on the website

Bus   PersepholisEND   BigBen

Chapter One

Fear Not

You have Photoshop on your computer. Perhaps you have had a play, got stuck, became frustrated, found the manual too technical and gave up! Here you will use real images to work your way through many of the tools and controls that initially seem so daunting – but in truth they are just buttons to press or un-press. If you make a mistake it is simple to go back. You will learn what the buttons do. Examples and projects demonstrate how these can be used productively and encourage you to think about the strategy of image manipulation. Initially Photoshop menus and tools may look like an aeroplane cockpit. Very soon you will find your way around. If you don't understand don't worry, you will be asked to repeat certain important techniques over and over. This book is intended to provide you with lots of ideas of what is possible and stimulate your own creativity. Once you understand the working process you can apply the same techniques to your own images. Some projects use scanned images, some photographs from digital cameras. Just one or two projects are created from scratch. Here you are introduced to some basics that you will need for the first few chapters. Strap yourself in and go!

Keyboard

Many of Photoshop's commands require you to press certain keys or combination of keys. Some keys like Alt/Option you may have never used before. Check that you know where to find these.

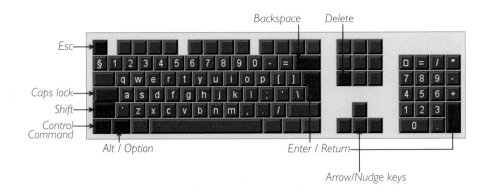

Understand your workspace

Title Bar

Minimize Maximize

Close

Menu Bar

Options Bar

Palette Well

Toolbox

Palettes

Palettes
Title Bar

File size

Photoshop in Windows

BEWARE

The colors you see on the screen may not be the colors you see when you print. More predictable results can be achieved if you set up a color workflow as shown at the end of the book. You can, however, complete all projects without doing this.

1 Open Photoshop. The workspace normally opens with a row of palettes on the right side and the Toolbox on the left. Move these around if you wish by dragging on their Title bar. If asked about Color Settings see the note to the left.

2 Close any unwanted palettes.

3 Open any file and note that it appears in its own window. Click on its maximize button to fill the screen or look at the choices available in the Options bar.

If you want to use the images shown here you can download them from the website www.ineasysteps.com. Save files in a specific location and consider making a folder especially for the exercises in this book.

Menus and Options

At the top of the screen is the Menu Bar. All computer programs have a Menu and most look similar to Photoshop,
File ... Edit ....Help

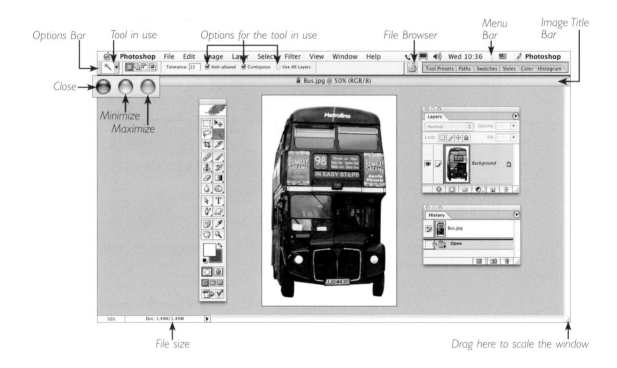

Options Bar — Tool in use — Options for the tool in use — File Browser — Menu Bar — Image Title Bar

Close — Minimize — Maximize

Bus.jpg @ 50% (RGB/8)

File size — Drag here to scale the window

Photoshop on the Mac

Position the Toolbox to the left of your work area so that it is not covered when other palettes open. Click on the Title Bar at the top of the Toolbox and drag it to the left of your screen. If Photoshop only fills part of the screen maximize the image window to fill the screen.

Open the file Bus. This is done through File > Open in the Menu bar. Maximize the image window to fill the screen and cover any distracting background. You should do this at the start of each exercise. It makes sense to use the whole of your monitor.

The Menu Bar never changes. File...Edit...Help etc... will always be in the same place. Just beneath the Menu Bar is the Options Bar which changes as you choose different tools. Pick different tools to see this happen. End up with the Zoom Tool.

Zoom Tool

At high magnification you see that the image is made up of little squares. These are picture elements or PIXELS – each one a specific color. All digital images are made of pixels. Whenever you change anything in a Photoshop image all you are really doing is changing the color of the pixels.

1 Pick the Zoom Tool. Move the mouse over the Bus image and the cursor changes to a plus sign (+). Click on the number 98, and the magnification will increase, in other words, you zoom in. Click again and again until (+) sign disappears. You are now at maximum magnification. In the Title Bar at the top of the screen the magnification is 1600%.

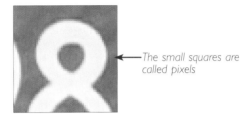

←*The small squares are called pixels*

2 Double-click on the Hand and the image reverts back to its original size.

If you cannot find a tool check the reference inside the front cover. Regardless of the tool you are using pressing the Spacebar will temporarily change the cursor to the Hand. You can then quickly drag around the image without changing tools or using the scroll bars.

3 Pick the Zoom Tool once more, but this time click and drag a box (called a marquee) around the name board. The precise size does not matter. Immediately you zoom into the area chosen.

←*With the Zoom Tool click and drag a marquee to quickly magnify a specific area*

In Photoshop 7 and later you also have the choice of using buttons in the Options Bar to zoom in and out. Since the Zoom will be in constant use get into the habit of using the keyboard shortcuts described.

4 Press and hold down the Alt/Option key. The plus (+) changes to a minus (-) and as you click the image gets smaller. If you persist long enough the bus almost disappears. Double-click on the Hand to restore the size.

Experimentation & History palette

© John Slater

The fun you have with Photoshop is largely due to the ease with which you can change, retouch and manipulate. You can do this to the complete image or to specific parts of the image. The parts are known as SELECTIONS. Much of the art and skill in Photoshop is being able to make good selections so that the changes you want will be specific and accurate. You will get involved with selections soon enough. For now, gain some confidence and experiment, knowing that you can make a mess and get out of it easily.

Image > Adjustments

1 Open the file Persepholis. You will make a few changes to this dark image. Remember, since there is no selection, all of the image will be affected. From the Menu Bar go Image > Adjustments.

2 Choose Brightness & Contrast. A dialog box appears. Move the sliders around and see how the image changes. Use the settings shown right and click OK.

Hue is color and saturation the richness of the color.

3 Look at a second option Image > Adjustments > Auto Contrast. There is no dialog box just an automatic change.

4 Try a third option Image > Adjustments > Hue / Saturation. Experiment but finish with the subtle changes shown right.

5 Next use Image > Adjustments > Color Balance.

6 Finally, go Image > Adjustments > Variations. This combines several options with the added benefit of a visual reference to any changes you may make. This is a great learning aid. If, for example, you are not too sure of "how saturation affects images", experiment with Variations. Choose an appropriate setting and click OK.

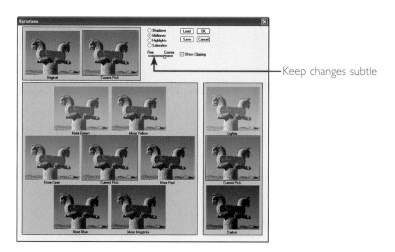

Keep changes subtle

Get out of Jail

As you experiment there is an ever present risk of making mistakes — it happens to everyone. Luckily each step of the process is recorded in the History palette. To undo a mistake or to simply go back to a previous "state" just click its entry in the History Palette.

 The History log is lost when an image is closed. In Photoshop CS the log can be saved as a text file.

1 The screenshot shown below shows a record of the changes you have made to the Persepolis image. To see this palette go Window > History. Click on the Color Balance "state" and step back to this previous version. Click on "Variations" and step forward to the present state.

 By default the number of entries in the History palette is 20. Increase this setting in the Preferences dialog box to at least 50.

2 To preserve a particular state throughout an editing session click on the Snapshot button.

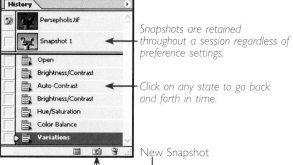

Snapshots are retained throughout a session regardless of preference settings.

Click on any state to go back and forth in time.

New Snapshot

Positioning Aids

© John Slater

There are several aids to positioning images and type in specific parts of a page. Visual placement is not always the best. Perhaps the easiest to understand is the Grid. This puts squares – like graph paper – all over the image. Use any image and from the Menu choose View > Show > Grid. In the example the grid is red and the squares are very close together. Yours may well be different. Change settings using Photoshop > Preferences.

On the Mac go Photoshop > Preferences.
In Windows go Edit > Preferences.

 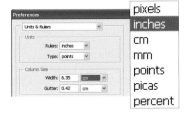

Under the View Menu there is also an option to make Rulers visible. First hide the grid and then go View > Rulers.

Along the top and left side of the image Rulers appear. The units (mm, inches etc.) can again be changed under Preferences. Change the units to inches. Regardless of the tool currently in use, put the mouse **inside** the top ruler. The cursor changes to a pointer. Click, hold down the mouse and drag downwards. This will drag down a horizontal guide. If you drag from the side ruler a vertical guide appears. Guides do not print.

You can have as many guides as you like and each one can be repositioned with the Move Tool. Guides do not print. If at any time you don't want to see the guides simply View > Show > Guides and untick the option. Change the color of guides in Preferences.

Move the mouse inside the ruler to drag a guide.

Rulers

Guide

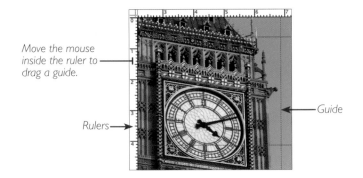

File Browser

Adjust the size of the preview from the View menu.

Small Thumbnail
Medium Thumbnail
✓ Large Thumbnail
Custom Thumbnail Size
Details

Making its first appearance in Photoshop 7 and considerably enhanced in CS is the File Browser. This lets you visually check all the images in a folder – no longer do you need to remember file names, and much frustration is eliminated! The Browser is now a powerful image management tool. Get to the Browser from the File menu, the Window menu or the Options Bar. Typically you would look through a collection of images with small or medium sized thumbnails of the folder contents. Then you could switch to Details view to give you more specific information. You can then view or add metadata and even use keywords to index or find images (see Chapter 4). Little things make the Browser easy and fun to use. One example is the ability to rotate images in thumbnail view, so that all images are orientated correctly. The "icing on the cake" is that Photoshop remembers this and whenever the image is opened, it is automatically rotated to the correct position. A nice touch! Explore and find how useful the Browser can be.

Try the PDF Presentation option to create your own slide show (CS only).

PDF Presentation...
Contact Sheet II...
Online Services...
Photomerge...
Picture Package...
Web Photo Gallery...

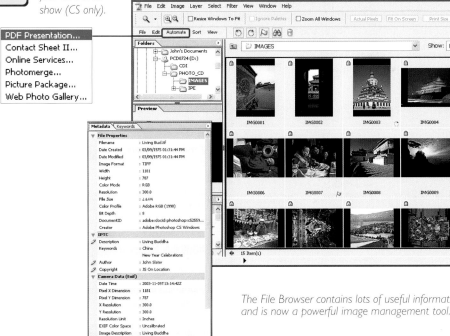

The File Browser contains lots of useful information, and is now a powerful image management tool.

Reset Tools

If the settings in the Options bar are not set to "Normal" many tools may not work as expected and, wrongly, you assume you are at fault. Many problems can be resolved by setting the tools back to their normal or default settings, using Reset All Tools.

Photoshop 7 onwards
Click on the tool icon in the Options bar

Photoshop 6 and older
Double click on the tool icon to bring up the Options box

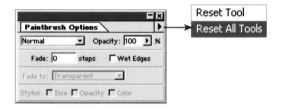

Help

There are times when things will happen and no explanation will be found on these pages. In this case try Help > Photoshop Help. Go and explore – you may be surprised how useful this can be.

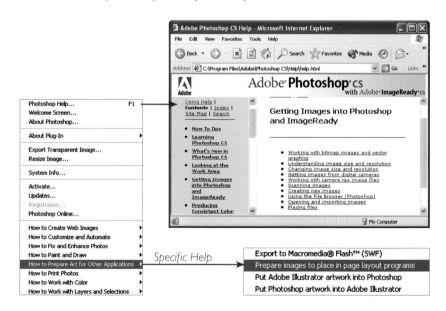

Projects with Layers – Basics & Fun

Of all the concepts in Photoshop the two most important are Layers and Selections. Think of layers as sheets of acetate or tracing paper floating over the image. Layers can be opaque, transparent or translucent. A selection defines any part of the image and restricts any actions to the selected area. Virtually everything you ever do in Photoshop will involve Layers and Selections. This chapter has three mini projects that encourage your understanding of layers and introduce you to selections. They are also fun!

Covers

This chapter uses these images

John   Painting 1   Painting 2   LibertyEND

Chapter Two

Introduction to Layers

© John Slater

This project takes you through three fun exercises, but beneath the fun is the understanding of the very basic and essential concept of layers. The first mini project simply involves re-creating a photograph of the Statue of Liberty that has been broken up into a number of "jigsaw" shapes. Each shape is on a separate layer and each layer has a number.

Open the file Liberty.psd and look at the Layers palette using Window > Layers.

The use of guides is strongly recommended to help alignment. Guides are discussed on page 18.

The translucency of a layer is controlled by the Opacity

Click here to turn off/on the visibility of a layer

Each section of the puzzle is on its own layer. The gray and white squares indicate transparency

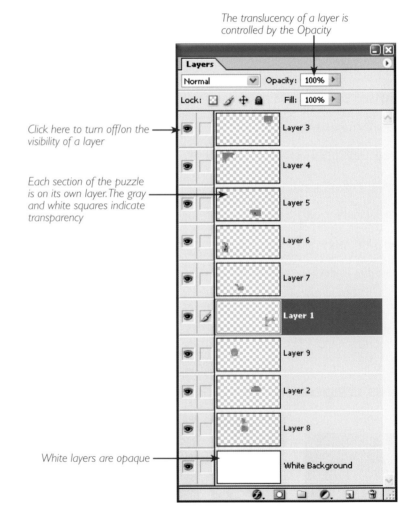

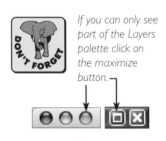

If you can only see part of the Layers palette click on the maximize button.

White layers are opaque

You will soon find it tedious to keep switching layers in the palette. Try clicking this button in the Options Bar.

Use guides (shown here in purple) to help align the different layers. The bottom left corner shape WILL be Layer1.

2   Click on Layer 1 to make it active and with the Move Tool position in the bottom left corner, using guides for reference.

3   Click on other layers in turn and with the Move Tool reposition each to reconstruct the original photograph.

4   Ensure that there are no white gaps between the shapes. If you find this difficult with the mouse, use the arrow keys to gently nudge the shapes into place.

Eliminate any gaps between the shapes. Arrow keys often allow more precise positioning than the mouse.

Crop Tool

Only flatten images when you are sure editing is complete. There is no easy way to go back. Flattened images occupy less disk space than layered images.

When editing is complete and you are happy with the result squash or flatten all the layers together. Although it is possible to achieve perfect results the chances are that your jigsaw will have some jagged edges. Crop the image to remove these and the white border.

1 From the menu go Layer > Flatten Image.

2 Pick the Crop Tool and drag a box (marquee) over the image.

Drag the handles to adjust the area to be cropped (removed). This is the area shown in yellow.

In older versions of Photoshop the Crop Tool lives with the Marquee Tools.

Crop box

Area to be cropped is shown here in yellow. It will be white on your computer.

Newer versions of Photoshop also have icons in the Options bar to accept or reject the crop. Enter and Esc keys work with all versions and are recommended.

3 Adjust the square handles to get exactly the crop you want. Press the Enter key to accept the crop, Esc key to reject.

4 Save the file as LibertyEND.tif.
   Go File > Save As. Get three things right, File Name (LibertyEND), File location (where you are saving the file) and File format (in this case TIF). If you are unsure about saving see the next page.

Saving Files

It seems obvious that you should save files in a location where they can be found. By default your computer will automatically take you to "My Documents" or "Documents". This is fine just so long as you appreciate what is happening. It is recommended that you make a folder for the exercises in this book. Consult your operating system manual for exact details but if you are using standard systems make a folder on the desktop as shown below.

Make a Folder

1. In Windows click on the desktop using the right mouse button. Then New > Folder. Name the folder and press the Enter key.

2. On the Mac press and hold the Control (ctrl) key, click on the desktop and then New > Folder. Name the folder and press Enter.

In the example below a folder called "Photoshop Exercises" has been created on the desktop

Once you have saved a file you only need to use File > Save to update any changes – there is no dialog box. If you want to keep intermediate versions of files use Save As and give a new name e.g. Liberty & LibertyEND.

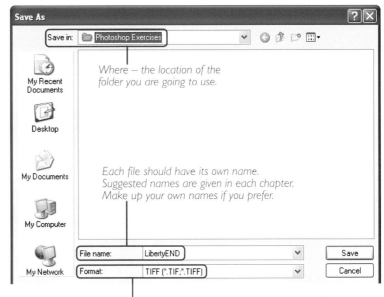

File Format – choose PSD, TIF or JPEG (see next page).

File Formats

Image files can be saved in a variety of formats. For the exercises in this book you only need to understand three formats: PSD, TIF and JPEG. The later is discussed in more detail on page 214.

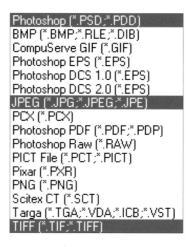

Photoshop 7 and CS allow layered files to be saved as tiffs – but this may cause problems with other programs. Play safe and save layered files in PSD format.

In the dialog box choose PSD (at the top). This is Photoshop's own format and keeps all layers intact – perfect if you need, or think you will need additional editing. Save the file.

Flatten the jigsaw file and File > Save As again.

PSD = Photoshop document.

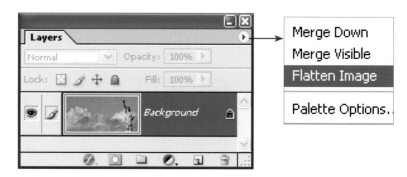

Flattened images have only one layer and this is called "Background".

Save as LibertyEND but choose TIF in the file format box.

"I didn't recognize myself"

© Adrian Paul

Another fun exercise to further your understanding of Layers. If you have a photograph of yourself it might be appropriate to use that – if not take one soon and repeat the project. Initially you need an image of a face looking more or less straight into the camera.

Prepare the image

You can change the size of the icons in the Layers palette using Palette Options.

1 As always Reset all Tools.

2 Open the file John. Yes it was a tough day!
Open the Layers palette (Window > Layers) – the image consists of a single layer called *Background*.

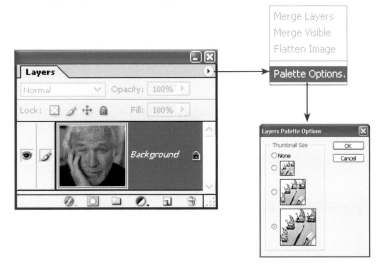

In the Rotate dialog CW is clockwise and CCW is counter-clockwise.

Drag guides from Rulers. Show Rulers from the View menu.

3 You may have heard that the left and right sides of your face are unequal in size. Prove it! Divide the image exactly down the middle as shown on the next page. It may be helpful to set up a guide to do this. With some images you will have to crop and rotate to get correct alignment.

This image has been cropped so that there is equal space left and right of the center guide. You may have to do the same with your own images.

...cont'd

To use the Marquee Tools simply click and drag to select the area wanted.

4 Make a selection with the Rectangular Marquee Tool of the left side of the image.

With the Rectangular Marquee Tool drag from the top left corner.

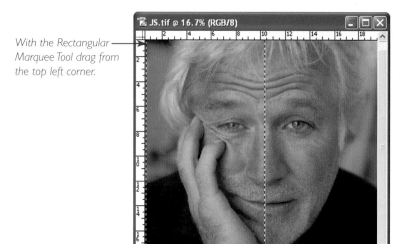

5 Then Edit > Copy. Follow this with Select > Deselect and then Edit > Paste. A new layer containing the copied selection is automatically created. By default this is called Layer 1.

If you don't deselect, the copied layer appears on the left and it is not obvious to see.

Change the name of layers to something more descriptive.

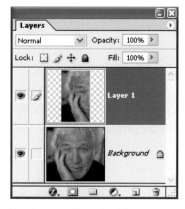

Your Layers palette should look like this.

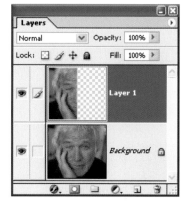

If you do not deselect before pasting you will not see any change in your image until the new layer is moved.

6   With the Move Tool reposition the half face to the right. Then, Edit > Transform > Flip Horizontal and a new picture is revealed.

 Return to the Background layer to make the selection.

7   Click on the *Background* layer to make it active and repeat the Selection > Copy > Paste routine for the right part of the face. Turn off/on the visibility ◉ of different layers in the Layers palette to see the three different images.

8   Save the file as JohnEND.psd. This format preserves the layers. Close the file.

 Always save the file in PSD format if you wish to preserve a image for future editing.

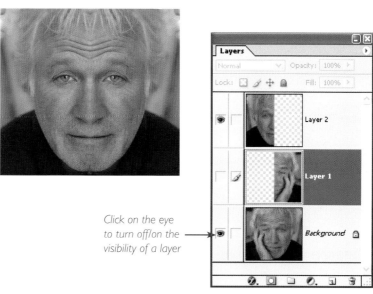

Click on the eye to turn off/on the visibility of a layer →

 If your starting images are not square the resultant images will have a more caricature appearance (see next project). You may lose a few friends!

Image not square?

© Malcolm Milburn

If you have a scientific mind and want to compare the two sides of a face it is important to have your subject square to the camera. If the images are not square then a caricature effect is achieved – which your friends may NOT thank you for.

1 Open the file John2. Not such a bad day! Make a selection of the narrow side of the face similar to that shown.

2 Repeat the procedure shown previously. Tidy up with the Crop Tool.

3 When you have stopped laughing flatten the image and save the file as John2END.tif.

Select the narrow half of the face, copy, paste, and flip horizontal.

More examples

Scanning large originals

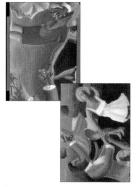

© John Slater

If you have a computer, and are reading this book, the chances are that you either own or have access to a scanner. Most "home-use" scanners will accept originals around 11 x 8 inches (approximately Letter size and A4) – so what happens if you have an original bigger than the scanner? The answer is to scan in sections and then seamlessly join them together. In this project you are asked to join two halves of a painting and make the join invisible.

Size Matters

1   Open the images Painting1 and Painting2. Don't worry that one of them is upside down – this is always likely to happen when you scan large originals. You may even find it beneficial to scan sideways.

Take originals out of their frames for scanning and avoid the strong possibility of false shadows and reflections.

2   Rotate the images so that they are the correct orientation using Image > Rotate.

In the Rotate Dialog box CW is clockwise and CCW is counter-clockwise.

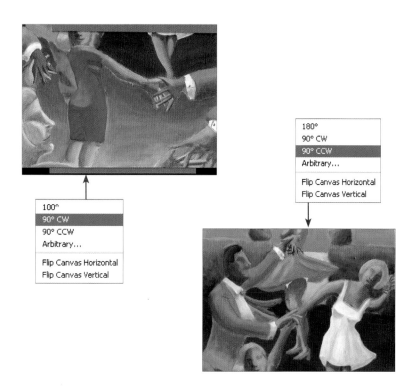

Move images side by side with Window > Documents > Tile (Window > Arrange in Photoshop CS).

No matter how many files you have open only one file is active. This file is indicated by a brighter title bar – non active files are dull.

Make room

You cannot just stick the two layers together. One of the files needs extra space to accommodate the other.

1 Make Painting 1 active (just click on it) and open the Canvas Size dialog box with Image > Canvas size. Here you can increase the space around the image and control where the original remains on the enlarged canvas.

The new space created on the increased canvas will be the background color shown in the Toolbox. In this project the color is irrelevant as it will be covered. In Photoshop CS you can choose the new background color.

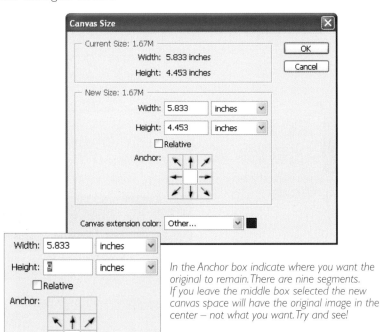

In the Anchor box indicate where you want the original to remain. There are nine segments. If you leave the middle box selected the new canvas space will have the original image in the center – not what you want. Try and see!

2 Take a careful look at the dialog box. Extra space is wanted above the painting but none at the sides. The Height box needs to be increased to approximately twice the setting shown – 9 inches is a good choice. There is no need to be specific – just make sure you create enough new space.

If you are confused about the terminology think of an oil painting. The Canvas is the whole fabric whereas the image is just the area covered with paint.

3 Select the bottom anchor square as shown. Click OK. New space is created at the top of the painting as shown next. If this is not the case, go Edit > Undo and try again.

Expect some variation in the density of a scan. This is likely to be more obvious with cheaper and older scanners. You may also want to include a section of gray card – or another known reference for easier color matching.

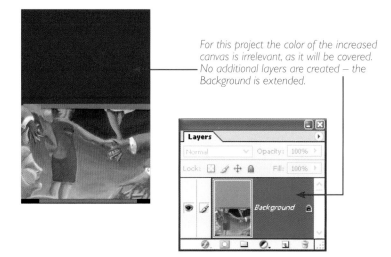

For this project the color of the increased canvas is irrelevant, as it will be covered. No additional layers are created – the Background is extended.

Assembly

When you drag an image to another file a new layer is created automatically.

Drag Painting 2 onto the enlarged Painting 1 with the Move Tool. Try and match them as best you can. With some originals you may have to use the Levels or Color Balance to get a good match. No matter what you do it is likely that you will still see a line at the join – especially in areas of lighter tone. Your first instincts might be to use the Rubber Stamp to eliminate this but, in this case, there is an easier solution.

It is very difficult to get exact alignment using the mouse. Use the arrow keys on the keyboard to nudge the images into place. Each nudge is one pixel.

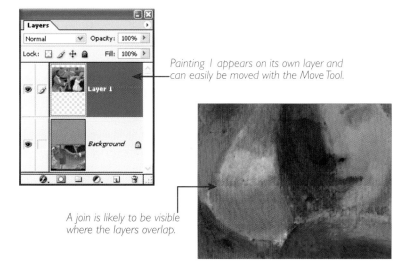

Painting 1 appears on its own layer and can easily be moved with the Move Tool.

A join is likely to be visible where the layers overlap.

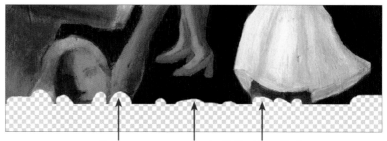

These areas are removed with the Eraser Tool.

Reduce the Opacity of the Eraser to make the blend even more subtle.

2 Remember that you are on two layers. Make the top layer active and with the Eraser Tool remove parts of the top layer where the join is obvious. Think clever. Erase in shapes e.g. with the face on the left erase the part of the cheek no longer required. In this way you can easily disguise the join so it is no longer visible.

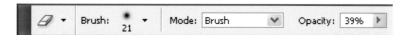

The size, shape and strength of the Eraser is controlled by the Options bar.

3 Flatten the two layers and tidy up the edges with the Crop Tool.

4 Save the file as MYPaintingEND.tif.

Remove unwanted canvas with the Crop Tool.

Color Line Drawings – Paint & Fills

Fill and painting techniques are important with all images. The first exercise in this chapter shows you how to add solid color to simple line drawings. Initially this will appear very easy. Quickly you will develop skills and techniques to aid productivity – techniques that you will use over and over again. In later projects you will learn how to grade and shade this solid color. Lastly a more creative, freehand approach to painting is adopted. The chapter also introduces basic skills with type.

Covers

Images to use & create

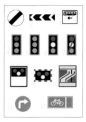

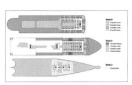

SignsEND   Boatplan   Broadway   Jockeys

Chapter Three

As easy as Painting by numbers

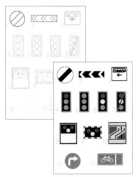

© John Slater

First you will color line drawings of very simple road signs. Then a somewhat more complex plan of a large boat. This could easily have been a garden plan, house or a simple fashion drawing. It is important to understand that for this simple technique the lines are all completely joined – there are no gaps. You will also learn the basics of adding text to images. All the signs were created in Photoshop.

Understanding default paint colors

1 As always Reset all Tools (page 20).

2 Open the file SignsLine. To see what you are expected to do you should also open SignsEND. Your task is to color the blank line drawings using the precise colors shown. Near the bottom of the Toolbox are two colored squares. Reset these to the default colors of pure black and pure white.

If you make a mistake immediately go Edit > Step Backward or use History as shown on page 17.

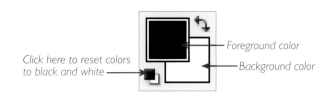

Click here to reset colors to black and white

Foreground color

Background color

3 Find the Paintbucket icon in the Toolbox. Zoom into the top left sign. Position the mouse cursor over the central stripe and click. The stripe is FILLED with black – the foreground color.

If you cannot see the icon you want it is hiding behind other tools. Refer to the drawing inside the front cover.

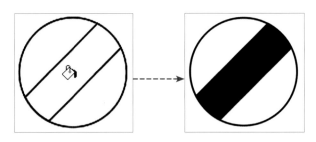

4 Repeat for Sign2 and 3. You will have to click several times to complete each. Don't worry about the text for the moment.

If you find it difficult to be accurate with the Paintbucket hold down the Shift key. The mouse cursor changes to a crosshair – the center of which is the aim point.

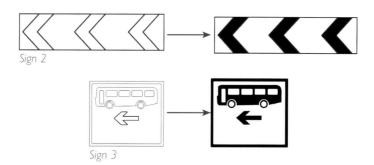

Sign 2

Sign 3

The Color palette

Zoom into Sign 4 – the traffic signals. Open the Swatches palette with Window > Swatches. You should see a standard set of colors. Use these as a painter would his palette.

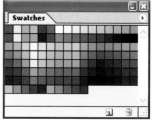

Refer to the finished SignsEND to see what the colors should be.

Click on the first red square and notice that the foreground color in the toolbox changes to this color. Anything you paint, type or fill will now be this color. The lower colored square is the background color and this will be discussed at a later time.

Fill the top circle with red. Change the foreground color to a mid gray and fill the bottom two circles and the surround. Finish with black. Repeat for Signs 5 and 6.

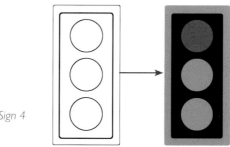

Sign 4

Signs 5 & 6

When you have a selection, a fill will only affect the selected area – other areas are not changed. Appreciate also that you know which areas are going to be filled with color. If you use the Paintbucket, by itself, this is not the case.

Remember the keyboard shortcuts. To add to a selection use the SHIFT key. To fill a selection use ALT + BACKSPACE.

If the Magic Wand is not working as you want, check the Tolerance or Reset the Tool.

4 For Sign 7 use a different technique. Choose a green foreground color. Pick the Magic Wand and click on the bottom circle. A moving dotted line appears just inside the circle. Many text books refer to this as "marching ants". It is correctly referred to as a selection. With the Paintbucket fill the selection with green. This may seem to be an extra process but you will soon see why making a selection first is strongly recommended.

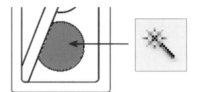

With the Magic Wand click inside the circle to make a selection.

5 With the Magic Wand select the outer frame. Choose a mid gray color but instead of using the Paintbucket to fill use keyboard strokes Alt/Option + Backspace. The selected areas is filled with gray. It is strongly recommended that this technique is memorized.

6 Areas of similar color can be selected and filled together. Make a selection of the red light. Hold down the shift key and notice next to the Magic Wand icon is a small plus (+) sign. Click on the red stripe and this areas is included in the selection. Press Alt/Option + Backspace to fill both areas at once.

Select these areas together ——

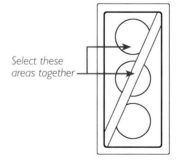

Sign 7

7 Continue with the other signs and save the file as MYsigns.

Type Tool – the basics [T]

Once the coloring is complete, finish the signs with some text. Photoshop now has very sophisticated type controls.

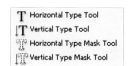

Make sure you are using the Horizontal Type Tool.

T Horizontal Type Tool
↓T Vertical Type Tool
🅃 Horizontal Type Mask Tool
🅸🆃 Vertical Type Mask Tool

1 Zoom into Sign 3. Pick the Horizontal Type Tool and click in the white space beneath the arrow to make an insertion point. A vertical pulsing line appears.

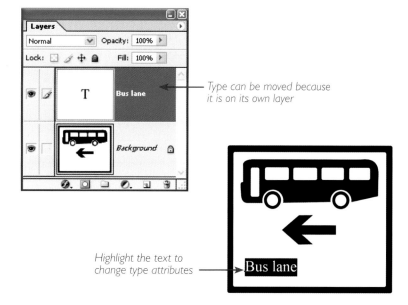

Type can be moved because it is on its own layer

Highlight the text to change type attributes

2 Type the words "Bus lane". Don't worry if the type is the wrong size or in the wrong position.

3 Reposition the text with the Move Tool ⊹ . To change the size, or the font, highlight the text and alter the attributes in the Options bar. Choose settings similar to those shown below.

4 Text attributes can be fine tuned. Open the Character palette,
   Window > Character. Highlight the text and change the AV
   setting to +50. The text spreads itself wider. Examine other aspects
   of this box.

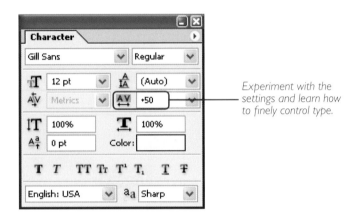

Experiment with the settings and learn how to finely control type.

Using type with Photoshop 5 & 6

The Text tool in older versions of Photoshop works in a different,
less intuitive, way. Pick the Text Tool and click on the image. A text
box appears in which you write the text and do any formatting
required. Click OK and the text appears on the image. To do any
additional editing double click on the type layer in the Layers palette.

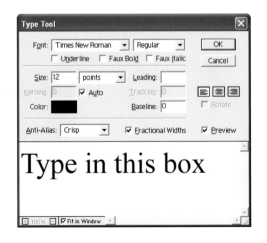

Custom colors

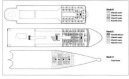

Original © Smyril Line

Slightly more challenging now. You will color the floorplan for a ferryboat. The exact colors you want are not in the palette but are shown in the key to the plan. You will add these colors to the Swatches Palette. Check out what you are expected to achieve by looking at BoatplanEND.jpg.

Open the file Boatplan. The drawing shows the deck plan of a ferry boat which travels across the North Atlantic Ocean to and from Iceland. Pick the Eyedropper tool . This samples color from any part of any image. Click on the bottom yellowish square in the key. The foreground color changes to this color.

> ## Deck 2
> ☐ Couchette

Move the mouse into the empty space at the bottom of the palette. Notice that the icon changes to a Paintbucket. Click and the yellow color is added. Name the color "Couchette". Repeat for the other six colors needed.

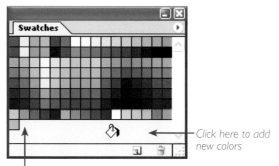

Click here to add new colors

New colors are added at the end. Give them appropriate names.

There are very many keyboard shortcuts in Photoshop. Alt + backspace to fill with color is one you should learn.

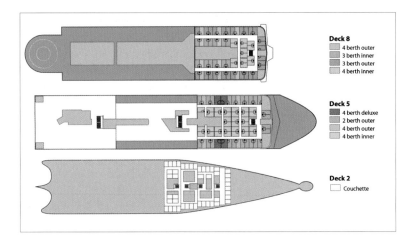

Swab the deck

1   Start with Deck 2 at the bottom of the illustration. Only one
     color is needed. Choose the pale yellow color that was previously
     named as "Couchette". Make sure that this is the foreground color.
     Pick the Magic Wand and make a selection of the little squares.
     Fill with the foreground color.

2   By now you should be getting the idea. Go through the rest of the
     illustration. Just follow the routine:

     • Make a selection
     • Pick a color
     • Alt + Backspace to fill with color.

     By the end of the exercise this shortcut technique should be
     firmly fixed in your head.

3   Save the file as MyPlanEND.

New clothes

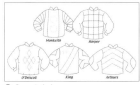

© Sue & John

This next project is typical of what any student or designer might do with images from their sketchbooks, magazine or book. Initially you will clean up the image and then add color and texture. Some of the lines are incomplete making selections with the Magic Wand impossible without a little "cheating". In later chapters you will learn techniques that allow you to make selections without cheating.

Eliminate unwanted text

Whilst you can use many images in books and magazines for educational purposes these cannot be used commercially without permission from the copyright holder.

1 Open the file Jockeys and Reset all Tools.

2 Unfortunately this image has been scanned upside down. This happens in real life – but is easily solved with Image > Rotate Canvas > 180°.

The Brush size is indicated by the mouse cursor. If you cannot see a circle, make sure the Caps lock key is not depressed, otherwise check Preferences.

3 The first task is to remove the text and the faint pencil lines. Pick the Brush Tool (Paintbrush) and a brush up to 100 pixel diameter.

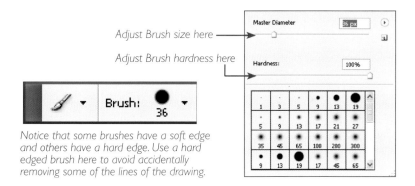

Adjust Brush size here

Adjust Brush hardness here

Notice that some brushes have a soft edge and others have a hard edge. Use a hard edged brush here to avoid accidentally removing some of the lines of the drawing.

Even though the background color may look white it may not be. Always use the Eyedropper to sample when exact color matches are needed.

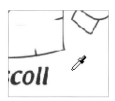

4 Sample the background color with the Eyedropper. Using the Brush Tool, paint over the text. Don't scribble, use smooth flowing strokes. If you make a mistake and remove any black lines, undo immediately, otherwise you may find the rest of the project difficult, if not impossible.

5 Save the file as MyJockeys.tif

Grade, Shade & Mode

Adding flat color should now be pretty easy. To make drawings appear more realistic shade and tone are needed. Here is a clever technique that is both useful and fun.

Set the Gradient Colors

1 Instead of a single flat color you will add a gradient of two colors to one of the shirts. The two colors will be the Foreground and Background colors. Select the first color you want from the Swatches palette. Click on the switch colors arrow and the chosen color now becomes the background color. Pick the second color and close the Swatches palette.

Some scanners automatically scan Black and white illustrations as grayscale or bitmap images. They will not accept color unless changed to RGB mode.

2 Confused? No matter what color you pick the Foreground and Background colors remain gray. This is simply because the image has been scanned as a grayscale image. In order to accept color, the Mode has to be changed. All images in this book should be set to RGB (red, green and blue), Image > Mode > RGB.

With grayscale images the foreground and background colors will always be shades of gray

The Gradient Tool may be hiding behind the Paintbucket. There are five Gradient Tools – make sure you pick the first one – the Linear Gradient.

Convert to RGB to allow colors to be added

3 Zoom into the shirt, bottom left.
Make a selection of the body with the Magic Wand.

4 Pick the Linear Gradient Tool – the gradient you have chosen can be seen in the Options Bar.

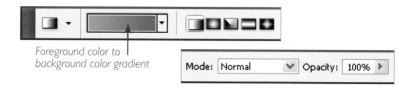

Foreground color to
background color gradient

Mode: Normal   Opacity: 100%

5   Click and drag the mouse across the selection. The area is filled
    with the set gradient. With the selection still active, repeat the
    process several times changing both the length of the line you
    drag and its direction. In this way you can control how quickly the
    colors change and the direction of the change. If you missed any
    areas with your selection, add them now and repeat the gradient.

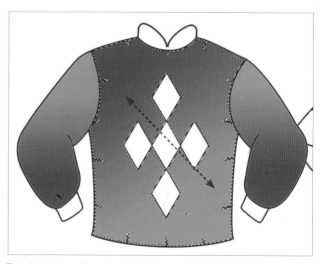

*The direction and length of the drag determine
the direction and subtlety of the gradient.*

*Select more than
one area using
the SHIFT key. Fill
using the shortcut
Alt + Backspace.*

6   Select both the sleeves and add another gradient. In the example
    shown the gradient is reversed simply by dragging in the opposite
    direction.

7   Save the file but keep the selection active.

Textures galore

Color added with the computer is usually flat and textureless. Tone is helpful, but textures make objects look more lifelike. Often the computer needs a helping hand.

You can undo any effect with Edit > Undo or reduce the effect with Edit > Fade.

1 Zoom into the sleeve of the shirt you have just colored and go Filter > Noise > Add Noise. Change the settings to see different effects, but end up with settings similar to those shown below:

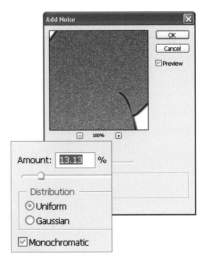

Once objects have textures or graded color they become more difficult to select. Try using the SHIFT key method.

When you are playing with filters it is easy to forget what you did. Note or photograph the History palette with a screen capture program for instant recall.

2 Noise makes other filters more effective. Go Filter > Brush Strokes > Angled Strokes. Adjust the settings, particularly noticing how the stroke direction can be varied. Click OK and save the file.

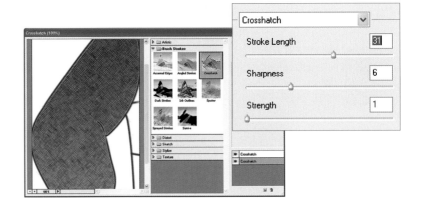

Line Cheat

This is not really cheating – it is more learning how to take control. With drawings that have incomplete lines or gaps new techniques are needed to control where selections are made.

1. Zoom into the top right shirt. Pick red from the Swatches palette and with the Magic Wand select the bottom right square.

2. Fill this square with red and work upwards filling every alternate square.

3. Fill the right sleeve. This also fills the top right square, which is fine. If, however, you color the left sleeve most of the background AND the top left square also fills – which is NOT what you want. This is caused by gaps in the drawing.

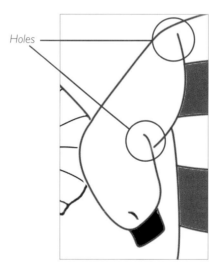

Holes

4. The remedy is relatively simple. Make a new layer. From the Menu go Layer > New > Layer. Name the layer "Cheat".

Ensure that you are on the "Cheat" layer.

5 Pick a very small Paintbrush (Brush Tool) and change the foreground color to black. Paint in the broken lines.

6 Here comes the trick. Pick the Magic Wand.
In the Options bar tick "Use all Layers".

7 Make the selection, make the *Background* layer active, and fill with color. Throw away the "Cheat" layer by dragging to the trash.

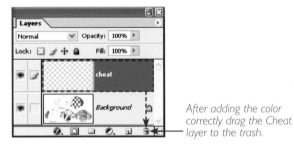

After adding the color correctly drag the Cheat layer to the trash.

8 Continue to color and texture the rest of the image.

Add shadows and highlights with the Burn and Dodge Tools.

Just my Type

Finish this illustration by adding some descriptive and creative text.

Photoshop 6 users and earlier will only be able to use "normal" type for this section.

Pick the Type tool and click anywhere on the image to create an insertion point. Type the word "Harper" beneath the red and white checked shirt. Check the options bar for font, font size etc.

Click on the Warp Text icon and choose the settings shown below.

Correct any errors in the type by highlighting the text and changing the options as in a word processor. Reposition any text with the Move Tool.

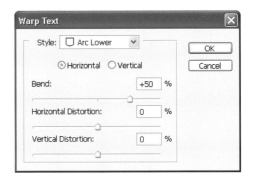

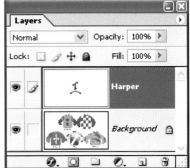

Type the other names and add similar settings. Flatten the image and save as JockeysEND.

Steal the show – Freehand Painting

© Sue Willmington

So far you have applied paint in a stylized way. The images you have used allowed this to happen. With less structured images a more "freehand" approach will often be necessary.

Never paint the original

1 Open the file Broadway. This is a line drawing with a limited amount of shading. The lines are joined up in places and this will allow selections to be easily made and filled. Where lines are non-contiguous (not joined up) selections, if wanted, have to be made by other methods or paint applied freehand.

This is a grayscale image. Convert to RGB with Image > Mode > RGB.

2 Some of you may be tempted to paint directly on the original – DON'T. Paint should be applied on its own layer, preferably a new layer for each area of color or tone.
Open the Layers palette. Rename the *Background* layer "Original". As an additional precaution, duplicate this layer as shown below.

← *Click here to duplicate a layer or make a new layer*

It is good professional practise to duplicate the background layer – just in case you mess up!

You may want to rename layers to avoid possible confusion. Double-click on the existing name.

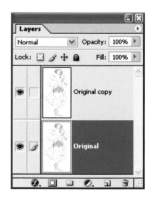

Brush stop

In modern versions of Photoshop there is a vast choice of brushes and an incredible, sometimes overwhelming, range of custom controls. Brushes are used with all the Painting tools, Eraser and Clone tools. Here is a brief introduction to the brushes palette.

1 Pick the Brush Tool (Paintbrush) in the Toolbox.

Click on the Brush arrow to reveal lots of choices.

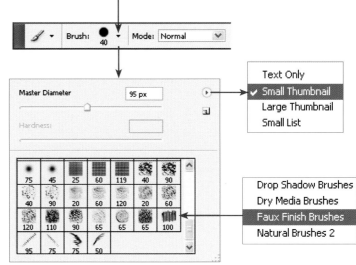

Early versions of Photoshop will have some but not all the choices shown here. To see the Brushes palette in v5 and v6 go Window > Show Brushes.

2 Click on the palette arrow and view the brushes as "Small Thumbnails". Append additional brushes.

In early versions of Photoshop additional Brushes can be found in the "Goodies" folder on the program CD.

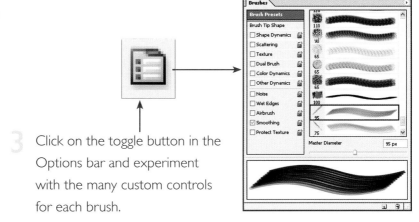

3 Click on the toggle button in the Options bar and experiment with the many custom controls for each brush.

Painting modes

Do not confuse new layer with duplicate layer.

Paint can be applied in many creative ways using the Painting modes. Their counterparts in the Layers palette are the Blending modes.

1 Make a NEW layer and name it Hat Color.

2 With the Hat color layer active zoom into the hat. Pick the Brush Tool (Paintbrush) and ensure that your options are similar to those shown below and do not change for the rest of this project.

Brush size Painting modes Strength of paint

3 Pick a mid-toned color and start painting the hat. Something similar to A will happen. This is obviously not what you want.

A. Normal

B. Darken

C. Lighten

D. Color

4 Change the Blending mode in the Layers palette to Darken and you will change the way in which the paint reacts or blends with the drawing. Your image will change to B. Try other blending modes, especially Lighten and Color.

Experiment with different blending modes

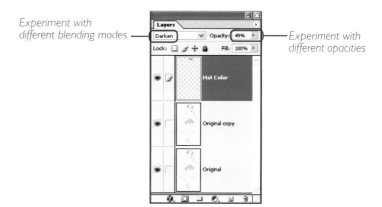

Experiment with different opacities

Use the paint blending modes when working on images with single layers. In this project use blending modes in the Layers palette.

5 Because the color is on its own layer this can be very easily changed at any time in the painting process.

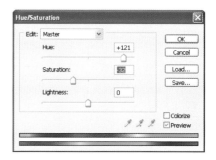

6 Similarly, paint on layers can simply be removed with the Eraser. Partially removing paint with textured brushes can add a tactile quality to your drawings.

Use the eraser at low opacity setting to blend and add highlights.

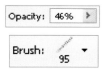

Remove unwanted paint with the Eraser

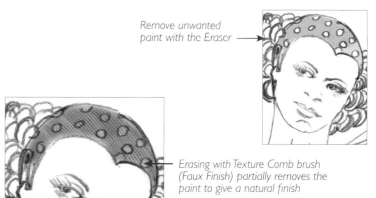

Erasing with Texture Comb brush (Faux Finish) partially removes the paint to give a natural finish

Add tone with multiple layers

Simulate tone by blending and merging layers together.

1 Make a new layer and name it "Dress". Paint the bottom of the dress with a pale color, similar to a wash with a watercolor painting. It does not matter if you do this freehand or within a rough selection.

If you name each layer "......color" this is a reminder that only color is applied to this layer.

2 Make another layer and name it Dress 2.

3 Pick a Paintbrush and with a darker or stronger color paint down the edge of each panel as shown below.

4 Adjust the blending mode and opacity of the layer as required. When happy with the result merge the two Dress layers together with Layer > Merge Down.

You can use filters on the colored layers for effect. Blur may be useful to help blend tones.

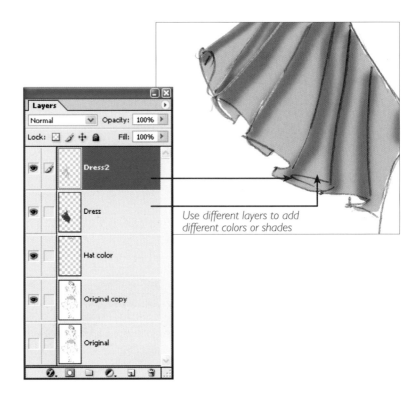

Use different layers to add different colors or shades

Easy selections with Quick Mask

Although you may want to paint freehand you may want to restrict the areas where paint is applied. The same technique also allows you to make selections of areas full of incomplete lines.

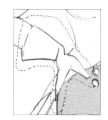

1 Zoom into the left glove and make a rough selection with the Lasso Tool.

2 Click on the Quick Mask button in the Toolbox to reveal the mask.

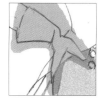

You can choose to have either the selected or the non-selected areas colored. To follow the example use the options shown. To get to this box double-click on the Quick Mask icon.

3 Change the foreground color to white and paint the mask (the pink areas). Using white paint will remove parts of the mask. If you need to add to the mask use black paint.

4 When the mask covers only the glove press the standard selection button in the Toolbox to revert back to a selection.

5 Fill or paint with color.

6 Change the blend mode if you want to see the pencil lines.

Create tone with Burn & Dodge

Somewhat simpler than building tone and shade with multiple color layers are the Burn and Dodge Tools.

1   Make a selection of the legs with the Quick Mask technique.

2   Make a new layer and fill the selection with a pale skin tone. Then Select > Deselect.

3   Pick the Burn Tool and set the options as shown below. "Paint" over the back of the leg and watch the tone gradually darken.

Keep this setting low

4   Switch to the Dodge Tool and work down the front of the leg to create highlights.

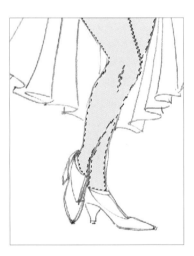 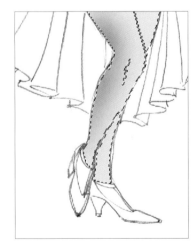

Keep the skeleton

In the process of selecting, painting, changing your mind and painting again, the black lines that make up the "skeleton" of the drawing start to disappear. There is a simple remedy.

1 Duplicate the original line drawing. In the example shown this is the bottom layer.

2 Extend the Layer palette so that all layers are visible. Drag the new copy to the top of the layer stack. Don't worry that it blocks out any previous work.

Change the size of the Layer palette icons with Palette options.

3 Change the blend mode to Multiply. If the effect is a little strong simply reduce the Opacity.

A duplicate of the line drawing at the top of the stack and a blending mode of Multiply will always reinstate any "lost" lines.

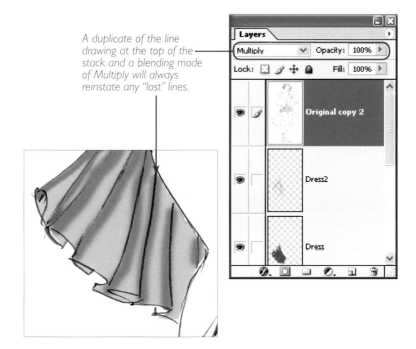

This last technique can be refined further using Layer masks (Chapter 10).

4 If you only want to increase the line density in certain areas use Layer masks as explained in Chapter 10.

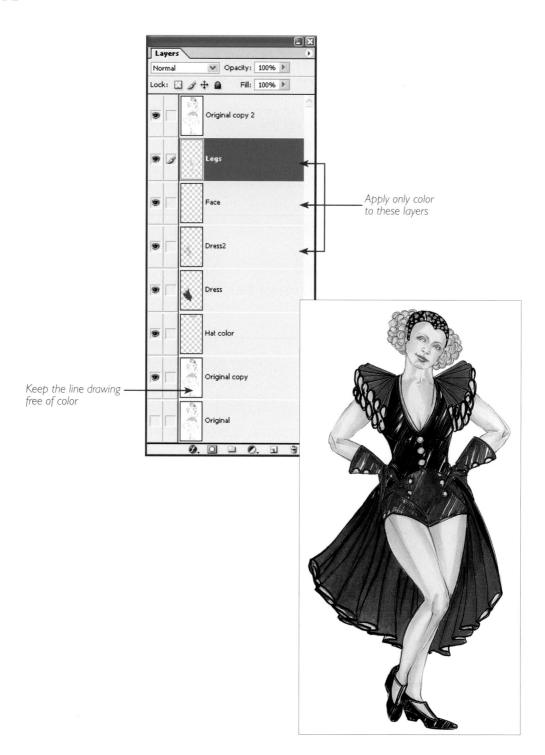

Apply only color
to these layers

Keep the line drawing
free of color

Image Correction – Basic & Creative

No matter how you get images into the computer it is more than likely that each and every one will benefit from some size adjustment, tonal change and/or color enhancement. This project demonstrates the basic techniques that can be applied to most of your images.

Covers

Images for this set of projects

Ice

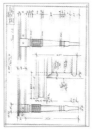
Table

Alex

Iceboat

Auckland

Chapter Four

On the level?

© John Slater

This project takes you through the basic stages of image improvement. The steps needed for correction to most images are:

Open
Crop and alignment
Global tonal change
Global color change
Local tone and color adjustment
Sharpen
Save

Undo / redo any changes by clicking on the entries in the History palette.

Perhaps the most important but the one that looks the most complicated (it isn't) is tonal change using Levels – so this is where you will start.

It's all in the graph

Open the file Alex. From the menu go Image > Adjustments > Levels. Initially some people might find this box confusing or intimidating but it is only a graph showing the distribution of pixels in the image.

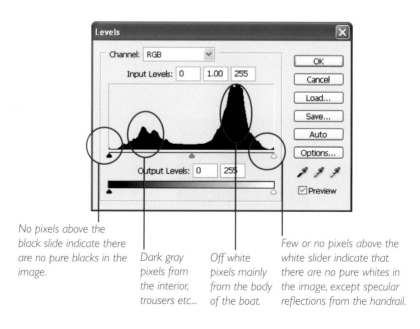

No pixels above the black slide indicate there are no pure blacks in the image.

Dark gray pixels from the interior, trousers etc...

Off white pixels mainly from the body of the boat.

Few or no pixels above the white slider indicate that there are no pure whites in the image, except specular reflections from the handrail.

2 With the Rectangular Marquee ⬚ make selections of small areas of the photo, in similar locations to those shown below. Check the Levels and start to anticipate the type of graph that will appear.

3 Once you understand close the file.

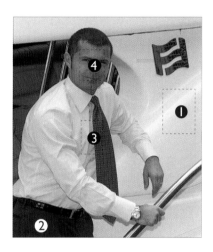

The dialog is opened with Image > Adjustments > Levels.

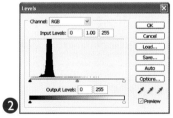

Only off whites

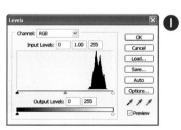

Only dark grays

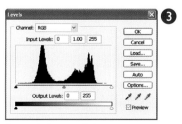

Some dark, some light tones

All mid tones

Test Run

1 Open the file Auckland and the Levels dialog.

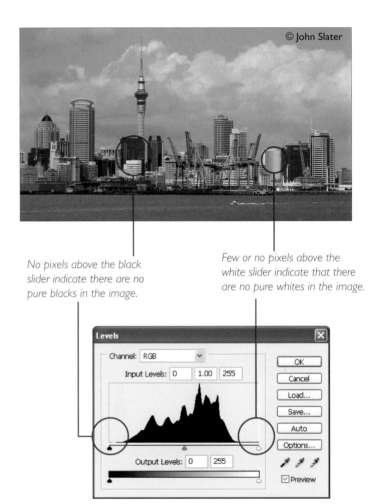

© John Slater

No pixels above the black slider indicate there are no pure blacks in the image.

Few or no pixels above the white slider indicate that there are no pure whites in the image.

If you make changes to the Levels sliders that you do not like press the Alt key to Reset, rather than moving the sliders back or pressing Cancel.

2 A good rule of thumb is to move the sliders inwards until the start of the graph as shown next. Immediately you will see an increase in contrast. This may cause some loss of detail in the mid tones so counter this by moving the middle slider – in this case a little to the left. The image should be vastly improved.

The closer the white and black sliders move to each other the more contrasty the image will become.

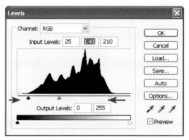

Before adjustment

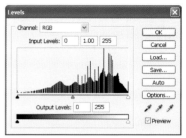

After adjustment

Image > Adjustments > Color Balance.

3 With any image personal choice is important. We do not all "see" the same. You should find, however, that this image has a pale blue cast. Reduce this by altering the Color Balance. If you are unsure get a better idea by looking at Image > Adjustments > Variations.

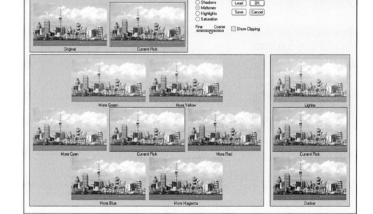

Keep the settings subtle.

4 Play around with this box to discover how the changes affect your image. Regardless of your own personal choice (in this instance) add more yellow and click OK.

5 If you find the result just too much don't backtrack but reduce the effect with Edit > Fade > Variations.

Use a soft-edged brush and keep the settings low and build up effects rather than trying to achieve finished results in one go.

6 The image should be looking pretty good but some emphasis to the clouds can have a dramatic effect. Pick the Burn Tool and with a brush about 60 pixels wide gently massage the clouds until they begin to stand out.

Keep this setting low

7 When satisfied with the changes save the file as AucklandEND and close. There is still one important job left to complete the image – sharpening. This is discussed later in the chapter.

Cool blues

© John Slater

Co-habiting with the Burn Tool are the Dodge and Sponge Tools. They work in the same way but have the effect of lightening areas and changing color strength – as you will soon discover.

1 Open the file Ice. The darkness you see is largely the result of underexposure – the camera was fooled by the unusual subject matter and lighting.

2 Open Levels and correct as shown.

When making subtle color changes ensure that your monitor is correctly calibrated (see page 225).

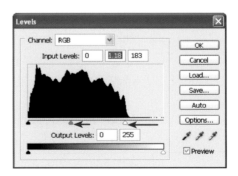

The Sponge has two settings. In this case you want to enhance color and not subdue it, so set to Saturate.

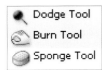

3 You may wish to darken the tones in the sky with the Burn Tool as you did with the Auckland file.

4 Enhance the feeling of drama by strengthening the blue of the ice. Pick the Sponge Tool and with subtle settings set to "Saturate" paint along the line of icebergs roughly across the middle of the picture. The blue becomes increasingly saturated the more times the area is painted over – and more accurately reflects the breathtaking impression when seeing the landscape for the first time.

5 Do the same for the small areas of lichen on the rocks – they should turn rich green.

6 Lastly pick the Dodge tool. Be very subtle and lighten the rocks and the inflatable boats to give them a lift. Save the file as IceEND, but do not close.

© John Slater

More control

Visual adjustment is all very well but some of you may prefer a more controlled method of setting Levels. Let's see how the computer can help.

1   Open the file IceBoat and Crop.

Crop the image to a more panoramic shape.

2   The file is low in contrast but has areas that could well be pure white and pure black. Open Levels and pick the white eyedropper at the bottom right corner. Click on the area you would like to see become white. There is an instant change.

The gray eyedropper causes color and tonal changes and should not be used unless you know you have a neutral gray in your image.

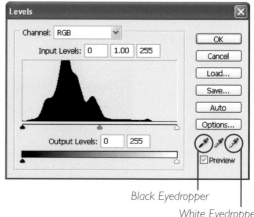

Black Eyedropper

White Eyedropper

Black Eyedropper is used to pick an area you want to be shadows.

White Eyedropper is used to pick an area you want to be a highlight. (Do not pick a bright glare or reflection).

Look at Levels after changes have been made and you will see a spiky graph. This is a sure sign that the image has been manipulated.

By default the white eyedropper is set to pure white and the black eyedropper to pure black. Experienced users can adjust these settings by double-clicking on the eyedropper.

3 Pick the black eyedropper and click on an area you want to be black.

4 The middle gray eyedropper should be used with caution, it is primarily a color correction tool. Only click on areas that you want to be mid gray – areas that you know are mid gray. If you are unsure it may be better to make a manual adjustment.

5 Finally increase the saturation of the image globally with Image > Adjustments > Hue/Saturation. Save the file as IceboatEND.

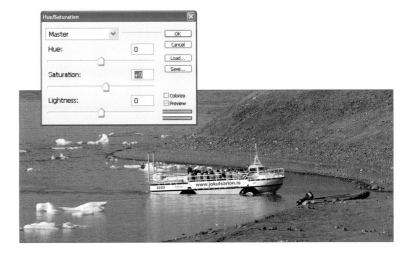

Sharp as a Razor

Sharpen after saving but before printing. This way if you make subsequent changes there is no adverse effect on the image.

Virtually all images will benefit from sharpening. The digital process softens all images. Look under the Filters menu and discover that Photoshop has four Sharpen options. The least obvious, but the choice of most professionals, is Unsharp Masking. The term is derived from a traditional photographic technique. Be aware that sharpening is normally the very last process before printing. The Unsharp Mask filter has three inter-dependent controls: Amount, Radius and Threshold. Experiment and experience are key to understanding these controls. Play around with the settings, apply to the two open files and save.

The higher the ppi, the higher the settings need to be to achieve a particular effect. Make selections and sharpen in specific areas to bring out fine details. The sharpening seen on your monitor will be more noticeable than on a print, where the inevitable spread of ink causes some image softening.

Threshold determines where sharpening takes place based on the difference in tone between adjacent pixels. At zero, sharpening will occur everywhere. At the highest setting of 255, only pure black pixels next to pure white pixels will be sharpened. Elsewhere there is no effect. A low setting (2–4) is normal.

Set the threshold value at 10 plus with portraits and avoid skin tones becoming mottled.

Radius controls the width of the edge created by the Threshold value. The norm for a 300 pixel per inch (ppi) image is 1–2.

The Amount setting increases the edge contrast, and a typical setting is 100% – 200%.

Cleaning

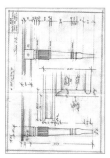

© Jamie Vartan

As you have seen, most scanned and digital files benefit from some tonal changes with the Levels command. The same controls can also have a creative use. Drawing paper and sketchbooks use paper that is often not white in color and may also have texture. Some of you will use tracing or drafting paper. All of these materials tend to scan very dark. This last section demonstrates two different techniques for cleaning such images. You are also introduced to Adjustment Layers and discover how adding metadata to your images can help in storage and retrieval.

Rotate, Crop and Straighten

Image > Rotate Canvas.

1 Open the file Table. This is technical drawing on drafting (tracing) paper and as you can see the scan is a disappointing gray. Additionally the scan needs straightening and some of the scribbled text etc. needs removing.

2 Rotate the image 90° CW (clockwise).

Use a guide to show the exact amount of rotation needed.

3 Pick the Crop Tool and draw a box around the edge of the image. Adjust the crop, then move the mouse OUTSIDE the crop box and rotate the crop as required.

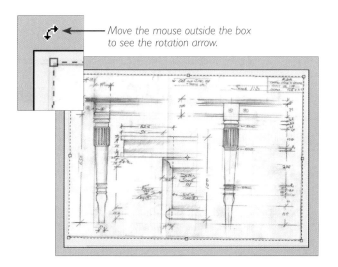

Move the mouse outside the box to see the rotation arrow.

Adjustment Layers

You will now eliminate much of the darkness in this image caused by the paper itself. Instead of using the Levels command from the menu adopt a more flexible approach with an adjustment layer. Adjustment layers let you experiment without making any permanent changes to the image. The changes appear as an entry in the Layers palette.

1 Open the layers palette and click on the adjustment layer button. Choose "Levels".

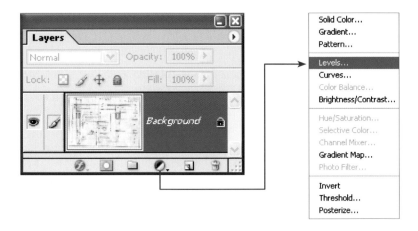

2 The normal Levels dialog box appears. Move the white slider to the left. The background is immediately improved. If you want you could move the black slider to the right to darken the blacks.

In this instance Levels are applied to the whole image, but remember you can make a selection and apply selectively.

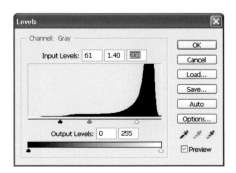

Move the sliders to similar positions to those shown.

Don't be greedy. Deep shadows and unwanted text are best painted out, otherwise fine detail may be lost. Some detail can be replaced using the History Brush (page 190).

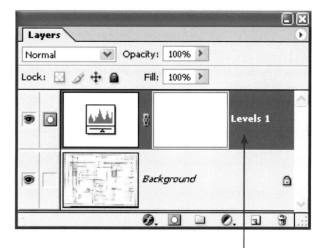

Double-click on the adjustment layer at any time to fine-tune the settings.

3 Make the bottom layer active and sample the background color with the Eyedropper . Paint out any additional unwanted detail as you did with the Jockeys file on page 43.

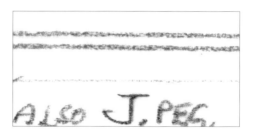

Paint away unwanted text and the double lines around the edge of the image.

4 When completely finished squash all the layers together with Layer > Flatten image. Save the file as MyTable.tif.

Two files are better than one

Every time you copy and paste, a new layer is automatically created.

The drawing includes detail of the table top at 1:1 scale. Remove this detail and make it a file in its own right.

1 Make a selection with the Rectangular Marquee and Edit > Copy.

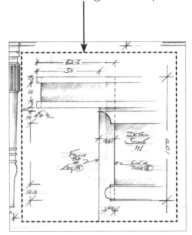

2 Now the clever bit. Go File > New. Accept the settings in the dialog box seen on your computer – these are exactly the dimensions needed.

The dimensions shown are dependent upon the size of the selection made.

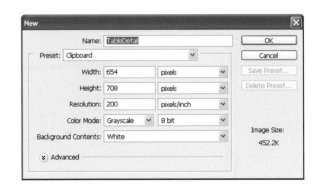

As an alternative to the Fill methods described earlier try Edit > Fill > White.

3 With the new, blank file open simply Edit > Paste. Flatten the layers and save as Tabledetail.tif.

4 Back to the Table file. The selection is still active. Fill with white.

Reposition the elements

Now that the file has been cleaned and detail removed, the two table legs can be moved closer. New clear type can also be added.

1 Make a selection of all the elements (other than the left table leg) with the Rectangular Marquee Tool.

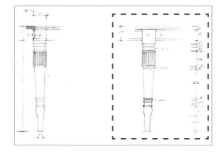

Ensure that the background color in the Toolbox is white, otherwise colors will appear when you move selections.

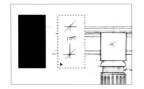

2 Switch to the Move Tool and drag the selection to the left. Tidy up with the Crop Tool.

3 Add some descriptive text and save the file as TableEND. Close the file.

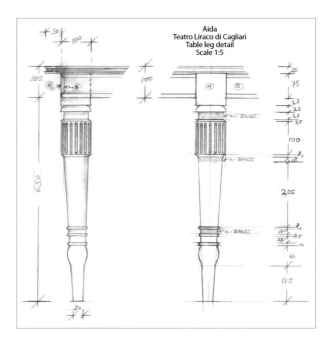

Metadata and finding files

If you are cleaning files for archiving it is a good idea to spend a couple of minutes adding some data about the image for future reference. This data will also help you find files.

You can only do this section if you are using Photoshop CS or later.

1 Open the File Browser .

2 Go File > Search, and in the dialog box enter the settings shown below. If you have downloaded the files for this chapter the search will reveal two files. Look at the metadata and keyword information.

3 Add some keywords to your own images and do another search.

Shortcut to the Search dialog

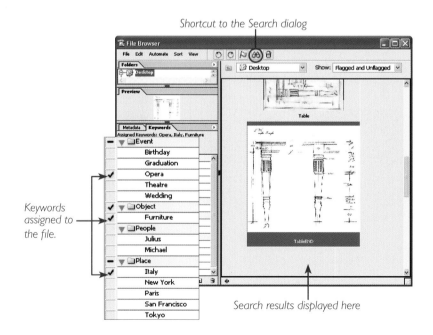

Keywords assigned to the file.

Search results displayed here

Perspective

Perspective creates the impression of depth and 3D. Photoshop can enhance perspective or correct distortion using the Transform commands. Particularly useful for architectural subjects but can be applied to any subject.

Covers

Images for this chapter

Canary

New York

Spa

Bank

Pattern

Space

Chapter Five

Perspective with Type

Everybody has seen pictures of buildings that appear to be falling over. This always happens when you tilt the camera upwards to take a photograph. Professional photographers use special cameras at the taking stage to correct this. Mere mortals have to resort to a little Photoshop trickery after the photo is taken. In the first project you discover how to take control of perspective with type.

Some Transform commands are not available with type unless it is converted into pixels – a process called rasterization.

Again
Scale
Rotate
Skew
Distort
Perspective
Rotate 180°
Rotate 90° CW
Rotate 90° CCW
Flip Horizontal
Flip Vertical

Basic Technique

1 Make a new file, approximately the dimensions shown below and type some text using a bold font.

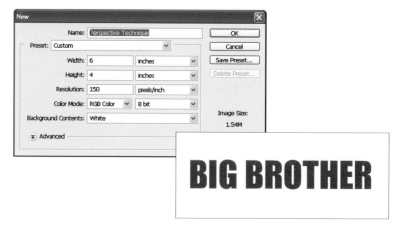

2 Type always appears on its own layer and is always identified by a capital letter T in the Layers palette. Rasterize the text to turn it into pixels with Layer > Rasterize > Type.

When type is rasterized it can no longer be edited.

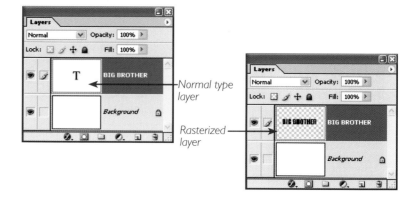

Normal type layer

Rasterized layer

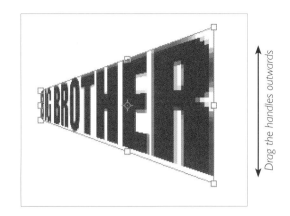

Drag the handles outwards

3   Change the perspective using Edit > Transform > Perspective. Square handles appear around the image. Drag the bottom right handle downwards. To accept any changes press the Return or Enter key.

In newer versions of the program transform changes can be accepted or rejected with buttons in the Options bar. In all versions Enter is accept and Esc (escape) is reject.

4   To increase the size of the text transform again with Edit > Free Transform and drag to the right.

5   Flatten the image and save the file.

Blurry?

You may well find that some of the letters become blurred by this process. This can be avoided by changing the text to a shape (Layer > Type > Convert to Shape) before transformation, and rasterizing only when necessary.

Transform shapes before rasterization and avoid jaggy edges.

Space Adventure – 3D Type

1   Make another new file and type "Space Ships" as shown below.

2   Rasterize the type then Transform > Distort. Adjust the handles to create something similar to the image shown below right.

3   Select the type with the Magic wand and apply a gradient – the example shows a Spectrum gradient.

4   Add depth by duplicating layers and moving upwards very slightly. Pick the Move Tool and hold down the Alt/Option key. Press the Up arrow key ↑ several times. Each time you press this key a new layer is created – in the example below some forty layers were created in just a few seconds.

5   Simplify the Layers palette. Turn off the visibility of the base layer and then from the menu bar go Layer > Merge Visible. Only two layers remain.

6   Save the file as SpaceEND.

Structural Engineer?

© John Slater

Apply your new skills to a photograph. Notice that the columns to the left are leaning outwards but the ones to the right look OK.

1 Open the file Spa and create a guide down the side of the left column to help alignment.

2 Duplicate the Background layer and Edit > Transform > Skew.

Guides are described on page 18.

3 Drag the bottom left handle outwards whilst watching the guide. Accept changes by pressing the Enter key.

4 Easy! Flatten the image and save as SpaEND.

The Transform commands are not available for files with a single Background layer. Duplicate this layer and the commands will be available.

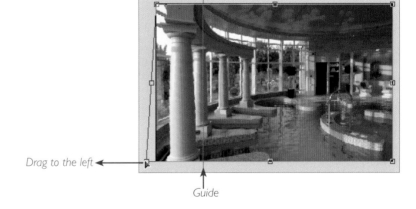

Drag to the left ←

Guide

In a hurry?

© John Slater

Sometimes you want to crop an image AND change the perspective. It is now possible to do both in one step.

1. Open the file Bank. Pick the Crop Tool and drag a marquee over the sign.

This technique is not possible with Photoshop prior to v6. Use the Transform commands described earlier.

2. Ensure the  ☑ **Perspective** box in the Options bar is ticked.

3. Drag each corner handle to the edge of the sign as shown below.

Drag the handles to the corners / edge of the sign.

4. Press Enter. That's all. Save the file as BankEND.

Please the Architect

© John Slater

You should be aware that using the transform commands will often cause the image to NOT look like reality. Sometimes this is fine if you are only trying to create an impression – as in the following project. The photograph was taken in the Docklands area of London.

1 Open the file Canary and duplicate the *Background* layer.

2 With the Transform commands straighten the building similar to that shown below using Edit > Transform > Distort.

Work on the duplicate layer. Compare images by turning off layer visibility.

Zoom out so that you can see all of the Transform box.

3 Compared to the original building the transformed image does not appear as tall or impressive as the architect would want. So make it bigger! There is no room above the building so make some space. Increase the Canvas size as shown next. Don't worry about the empty space created at the top of the frame.

...cont'd

Don't worry about this space
– it will soon be gone.

 If you are not good with numbers use the percent setting – you only need to be approximate.

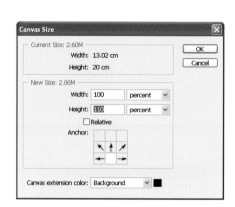

4 Go Edit > Free Transform. Drag one of the top handles straight up to the top of the frame. Press Enter to accept the changes.

5 Flatten the image and save as CanaryEND.psd.
The image is distorted but can you tell?

Distort the Truth

© John Slater

Sometimes distortion becomes unrealistic. In the following example you will see how bad it can get – only you can be the judge if this is acceptable or not.

1 Open the file New York and duplicate the Background layer.

2 Use Edit > Transform > Distort to eliminate most of the architectural distortion.

3 Compare the two layers by turning off/on the visibility of the top layer.

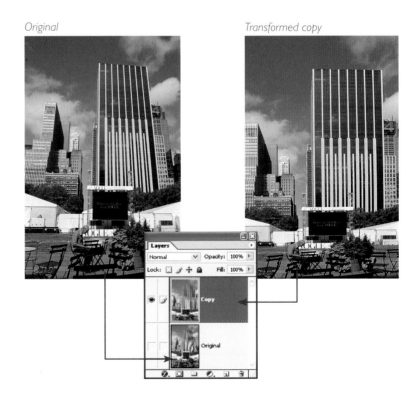

Original   *Transformed copy*

Click on the eye to make layers invisible.

4 The distortion causes the building to look smaller and fatter. Correct this by stretching the top few floors.
With the Rectangular Marquee select the top third of the image and Edit > Free Transform.

5 Drag the middle handle upwards as shown below.
Only you can judge if the truth is being distorted too much.

Drag upwards to make the building taller.

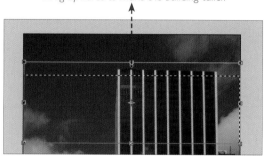

© John Slater

Continue the Fantasy

Accept the transformation and deselect. Move further away from
reality by putting a new image into the big screen.
Open the file FashionShow. Select > All, then Edit > Copy.
Close this file as it is no longer needed.

*When an image
is copied it is
temporarily stored
in computer
memory.*

2 Make a selection of the screen with the Polygonal Lasso and
Edit > Paste Into. A new layer is created automatically.
Rename this layer "Fash".

3 Adjust the scale as you wish with Edit > Transform > Scale.
In the example the image has also been flipped.

*Zoom out to
see all of the
Transform box.*

...cont'd

If you want to make the pattern yourself refer to page 216 for details.

LinePattern.tif

All the working images associated with this book are RGB files, and so have 3 channels, Red, Green and Blue.

The file LinePattern.pat can be found on the website.

4   To make the screen look more realistic create some lines over the new image. Do this using the image LinePattern.

5   Make a new layer and call it "Pattern". Reselect the screen and Edit > Fill. Change the "Use" box to Pattern.

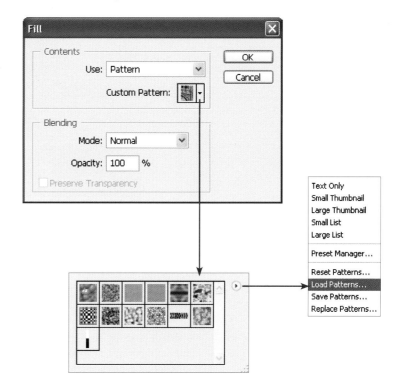

6   Click on the Custom Pattern arrow and then the library palette arrow. Choose Load Patterns. Find LinePattern.pat and it will appear in the pattern library.

7 Choose the new pattern and click OK. The striped pattern appears over the screen. Reduce the Opacity of this layer and, maybe, change the blending mode. Save the file as MyNewYork.

Dolly the Sheep – Retouching projects

Dirt, scratches, dust are all enemies of any photograph. Photoshop has many allies is this war against unwanted marks – but they also have many creative strengths that will charm you. Collectively these are the Clone Tools. This series of projects introduce a variety of techniques that extend from the simple removing of marks on photographs to transplanting body parts.

Covers

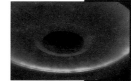

Spasky

Malc

Images for these projects

MuckyMilly   Balloons   Liz   Pool

Chapter Six

Repair, Restore and Mend

© John Slater

All types of images, photographs, paintings etc. are prone to damage, abuse and degradation. Until very recently the remedy for this was to restore by cleaning or painting the original. With digitalization, a better alternative is available. The tools you will use are the Clone Stamp and the Healing Brush. They work in a similar way – define an area and copy this, in real time, to another area. There is a knack to getting this right and good results will require you to experiment with lots of images.

Make basic corrections (as well)

1 Reset all Tools and open the file MuckyMilly.

2 Even though this project is about cloning it doesn't mean that you escape the important and necessary task of basic image correction. Suggested changes are shown below.

Versions of Photoshop older than v6 only have the Clone Stamp, but you can still do everything asked in this project.

Crop and rotate

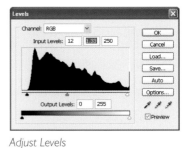

Adjust Levels

Make global color adjustments

Desaturate red face

Clone Stamp Tool

Zoom into the top right corner. There are quite a few dark blobs. Pick the Clone Stamp Tool and set the Options as shown below.

If you get an error message you have not pressed the Alt/Option key correctly.

Position the mouse just to the right of the darkest blob. Press the Alt/Option key (the mouse cursor will change) and click with the mouse. This defines the area you want to copy from – the source.

Each mouse click creates an entry in the History palette, so it is easy to undo any mistakes.

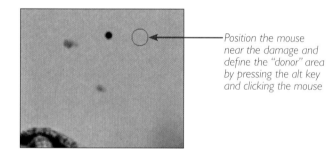

Position the mouse near the damage and define the "donor" area by pressing the alt key and clicking the mouse

Move the mouse over the black blob and click. If you hold down your mouse you will see a circle and a cross as shown below.

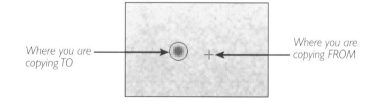

Where you are copying TO

Where you are copying FROM

Resample lots and lots of times to avoid the build up of patterns. Try and match the damaged areas perfectly. If you find the face difficult, undo your efforts, change the Mode to "Darken" and try again.

The black blob should disappear. If not quite complete just click again. Repeat the whole sequence for the other two blobs.

Move to the face and remove the white marks.
A little more care and smaller brushes will be needed.

Already an expert

Move your attention to the long white mark to the right of Milly's head. Ideally this will be removed in a single mouse stroke.

1 Position the mouse very near to the top of the white line and define the source area (Alt/Option + Click).

2 Move the mouse over the line. Whilst holding down the mouse drag over the line all the way to the end.

You can have even better results by changing the Mode in the Options bar.

Mode: Lighten
Lighten mode will only change pixels darker than the source.

Mode: Darken
Darken mode will only change pixels lighter than the source.

3 Touch up any other areas that are not quite perfect – probably the hair.

This is relatively easy because the background is diffuse and the colors mix well. If, however you look at the trousers, near the pocket, there is a line of black marks over the corduroy fabric texture. Here a little more care is needed.

4 Position the mouse close to the top of the marks and define the starting point as one of the darker stripes.

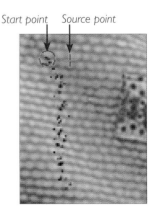

5 Move over to the marks and check your positioning by pressing the Alt/Option key (by itself). When you are aligned correctly over the mark and ON the black line click and drag as previously.

6 Tidy up any stray marks and save the file as MillyEND.

Disappearing trick

© John Slater

So long as you appreciate that pixels are being copied, not removed, this is an easy technique to understand. You are going to "eliminate" the text on a poster. Take plenty of time to do this.

1. Open the file Balloons and zoom into the text. Pick a suitably sized brush (about 13 pixel) and define a source point just below the hyphen (between 9–5), as shown below.

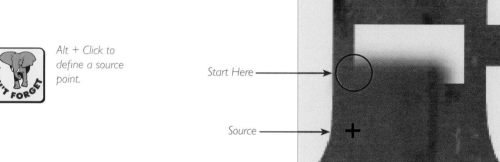

Start Here

Source

Alt + Click to define a source point.

2. Move the mouse over the bottom of the hyphen, click and drag to the left. The action "reveals" more of the colored background.

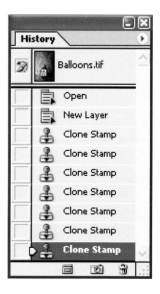

Resample frequently. You should see multiple entries in the History palette. Always work from the edges to the center. Try multiple clicks instead of "painting".

3. Resample many different areas and clone until all the text is gone and you have a good looking background largely restored. If patterns start to appear undo using the History palette.

Rope Trick

Layer > New > Layer.

The only tricky bit is the string. If you try a straightforward clone the chances are the new areas will not be aligned correctly – try it and see. You can overcome this by cloning onto a new layer and then rotating this layer to fit.

1 Make a new layer, name it "String". Return to the Background layer to define the source point exactly on the left string.

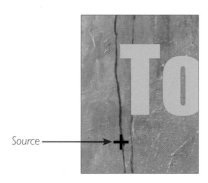

Source ——

2 Make the String layer active and clone, dragging upwards. Check your work by turning off the visibility of the *Background* layer.

3 Move the "new" string into position and align using Edit > Free Transform. Save the file as BalloonsEND.

Move the cloned string, you will need to transform this to make it appear realistic.

Rotate the String layer for a perfect fit. Do this by positioning the mouse OUTSIDE the transform box and then moving the mouse. ——

Healing Brush

© John Slater

The picture for this project may look like the Starship Enterprise, but it is the amazing ceiling of a hotel spa in Southern England. Unfortunately the high humidity caused condensation on the CCD of the digital camera and resulted in lots of dark spots over the image. Eliminate these with the Healing Brush.

CCD refers to Charge Coupled Device – the film of digital cameras.

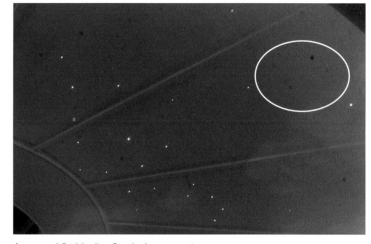
Area used for Healing Brush demonstration

If your version of Photoshop does not have the Healing Brush use the Clone stamp.

1 Open the file Spasky and zoom into the top right corner to see the mess that has been created. You could use the Clone Stamp but if you have it use the Healing Brush. For the sake of illustration concentrate on the ceiling panel at the 2 o'clock position as shown above.

2 Define a source area using the same Alt + Click method used for the Clone Stamp, and stroke over two or three spots at once. If you observe carefully you will notice that the computer takes a fraction of a second to "think" before making any changes. There is a blend of tone, color and texture between the donor and the recipient areas. Expect the blend to be superb.

You can achieve even better results by changing the Mode in the Options bar.

Mode: Lighten

3 Continue to remove the numerous marks, but avoid areas of high contrast – they pose their own problems.

The way the tool works is also one of its weaknesses. In areas of similar tones, similar color, or similar contrast the tool works very well. However, in areas of high variation blurring can result unless you change your working method as shown below.

Do not use the Healing brush in areas of high contrast or strong color variation – blurred results are almost certain.

Make the selected area bigger than the damage to allow better blending.

4 Zoom into the areas just above the windows and use the tool. Unless you change the blending mode the result will be blurred as shown right.

5 If you do not wish to continually change the blending mode, make a selection with the Lasso Tool around the defective area. This will stop the computer using the nearby areas of different tone and contrast to evaluate the finished result. If you remove all the remaining marks you will be well on the way to becoming an expert with this tool. Save the file as SpaskyEND.

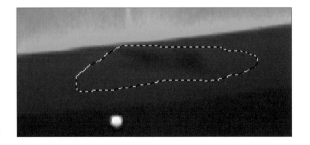

Plaster over the faults

© John Slater

Use a variety of retouching tools to create an image worthy of appearing in a company brochure. In this project you need to fix all the lights that are not working, remove the ventilation ducts, the odd sign and enhance a few other features!

1 Open the file Pool. Duplicate the *Background* layer and correct the perspective using Edit > Transform.

2 With the Clone Stamp Tool remove the 5 ventilation grills in the ceiling.

Always work on a copy layer but merge layers to keep the Layers palette simple.

3 Select one of the working ceiling lights with the Lasso Tool and duplicate this onto its own layer with Layer > Layer via Copy. Name the new layer "Ceiling light".

You may need to do a small amount of cloning in the bottom right corner.

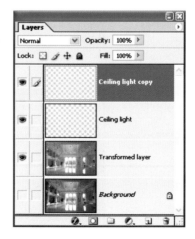

Be professional and give layers meaningful names.

4 Move the copy and cover one of the lights that is not illuminated. Repeat for the other light. You may need to use the transform commands to adjust the scale.

Additionally there are 2 wall lights that are not working. Copy–Paste or the Layer via Copy command does not give a great result (try it!). Instead clone across layers as previously with the Balloons image.

5 Suggested settings for the cloning are:

6 The cloned areas are the wrong size. Correct these using the Transform commands, and perhaps reduce the opacity in the Layers palette. Appreciate that this would be impossible to do if you had cloned directly onto the original.

7 Duplicate the transformed wall light layer and replace the last remaining non-working light. Save the completed file as PoolEND.

Transform the cloned reflection to make it bigger.

If you make any changes to the model don't forget the reflections.

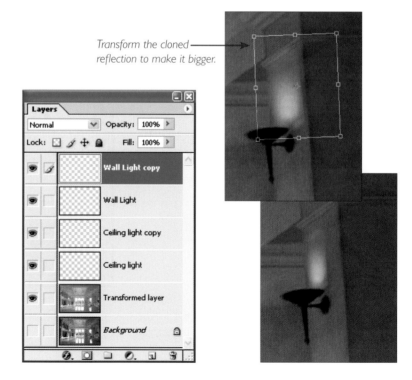

Face up to it

© John Slater

The Clone Stamp and Healing Brush are great for getting rid of spots and freckles. Here you use these tools in a more powerful way to enhance a model dressed to look like Queen Elizabeth1. Additional new techniques are needed to complete the transformation. You have to:

• Smooth and lighten the face
• Change the hair color
• Refine the lips

What wig?

1. Open the file Liz and zoom into the forehead. Notice that the model is wearing a wig and that the join is too obvious. Use the Clone Stamp or Healing brush to eliminate this as seen previously. A few sweeps with a large brush should be enough.

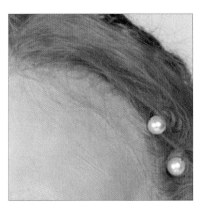

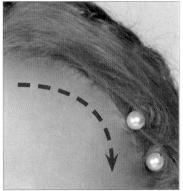

2. Don't worry if the edges between the face and hair are a little obvious – this will be remedied at the end of the project. Save the file as MyLiz.psd (File > Save As).

Refine the lips

Look carefully and you will see that the make-up has attempted to reduce the size of the lips. A slight "ghosting" remains. You will use both the Healing Brush and the Clone Stamp tool to eliminate this ghosting.

The Clone Stamp tends to cause softness, whereas the Healing Brush preserves texture.
In areas of variable contrast the Healing Brush causes a color blur – hence the need for either a selection and/or prior use of the Clone Stamp.

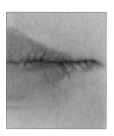

1 Make a selection of the lips with the Lasso Tool .

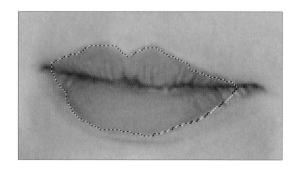

2 Select just the face with Select > Inverse.

3 Soften the selection with Select > Feather.

4 Make a broad sweep with the Clone Stamp Tool around the bottom lip. If available repeat the action with the Healing Brush.

5 Update the saved file with File > Save.

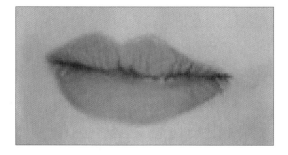

Red Head

From historical accounts it is clear that Elizabeth had red hair, but the model does not. Try your hand at being "Vidal Sassoon".

1 Make a new layer and call it Hair Color.

2 Click on the foreground color to open the Color Picker. Choose a suitable orange-red color.

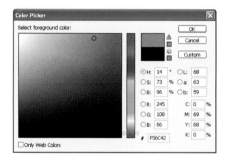

3 With a large soft brush make a broad sweep over the hair. Don't panic yet!

4 In the Layers palette change the blend mode to color and significantly reduce the opacity. Hey Presto!

5 Use the Eraser to remove any stray paint at the edges of the hair. With a very small brush click on the pearls to return them back to their natural color.

Elizabethan facial

Having a tan was not always regarded as fashionable. In the Elizabethan period pale skin distinguished nobles from the "peasant" who worked outside in the sun. The following technique not only softens and smooths skin but facilitates simple changes in tone.

Use the tools in combination. Press and hold the Shift key to add to the selection or the Alt key to remove from a selection.

1   Use a combination of the Lasso Tool and the Magic Wand to make a rough selection of the face and neck similar to that shown right. It is NOT essential to keep the eyes and lips free of the selection.

2   Copy the selected area onto its own layer. The neat way is Layer > New > Layer via Copy.
A new layer appears in the Layers palette.

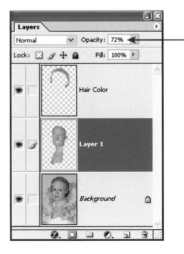

Lower the Opacity of Layer 1 so that some of the structure and texture of the underlying layer shows through.

3 Soften and smooth this layer with Filter > Blur > Gaussian Blur. Reduce the Opacity of this layer so that a hint of the underlying original is visible.

4 Lighten the skin with Image > Adjustments > Hue/Saturation.

If the skin looks too "pancake" add very gentle texture with Filter > Artistic > Film Grain.

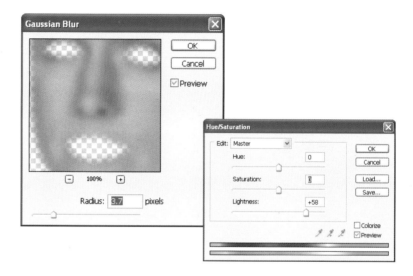

5 Pick the Eraser Tool and at low opacity work over important features such as the eyes, mouth and nose so that a little more of the underlying sharpness is revealed. Change the opacity to maintain a smooth blend. Save the file.

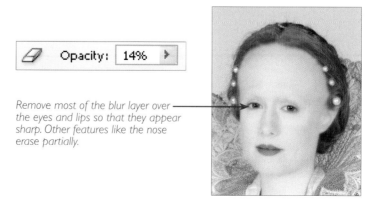

Remove most of the blur layer over the eyes and lips so that they appear sharp. Other features like the nose erase partially.

Finishing touches

To finish off make the lips stronger in color, add a hint of blusher and blend the wig line.

Control the paint flow from the airbrush with the mouse – just like a spray can.

HOT TIP

1 Make a new layer and call it "Lips". Change the blend mode to Color or Color Burn. Pick a strong red and apply paint over the lips. If the effect is too strong simply lower the layer opacity.

2 Make another new layer and name it "Blush". Pick the Airbrush (Brush Tool) and set the options as shown below. Apply subtle, smooth paint as required.

Press this button to use the Airbrush

3 Either flatten the image or move to the *Background* layer. Pick the Blur Tool and work around the hair line to disguise any remaining imperfections. Save the file.

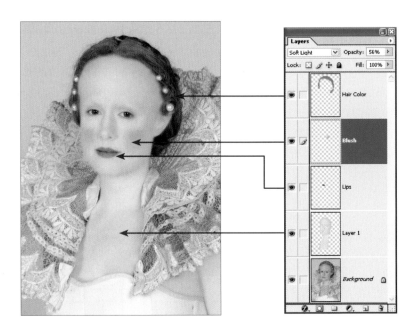

Steal body parts!

© John Slater

Sometimes you take a photograph and it just doesn't work – somebody moves their head, a stranger gets in the way, or people close their eyes. In this last section on retouching you are shown how to borrow eyes from one picture and insert them in another.

1 Open the files Malc1 and Malc2. Arrange them so you can see both images. Malc1 is the image you want to use but with the eyes from Malc2.

2 Pick the Lasso Tool and make a rough selection around the eyes of Malc2.

3 With the Move Tool drag the selection onto Malc1.
A new layer is automatically created. Close the Malc2 file as it is no longer needed.

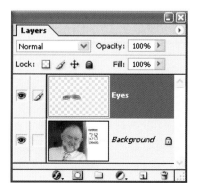

4 The eyes are the wrong size and have slightly the wrong orientation. Correct these with Edit > Transform > Scale and Edit > Transform > Rotate.

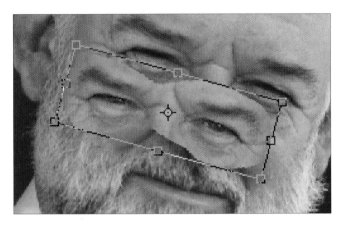

5 The skin around the eyes is the wrong color. Correct this with Image >Adjustments > Color Balance.

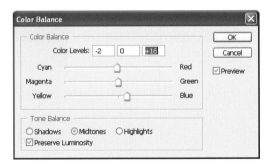

6 Blend the two layers together. Pick the Eraser Tool and set the Options as shown below. Repeatedly work around the eyes erasing or partially erasing the unwanted skin and the two layers start to blend together.

Eye surgery

The finished result isn't bad but Malc appears not to be looking at the camera.

1 Edit > Transform > Flip Horizontal to turn the eyes towards the camera. You will have to reposition and do a little more blending.

2 To enlarge the eyes a little further try the Liquify filter. Go Filter > Liquify. Be subtle!

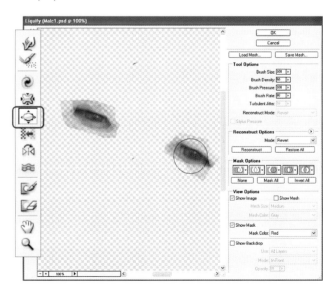

3 Try the settings shown first. All you need is a very, very gentle click with the Bloat Tool on each eye.

4   Click OK and look carefully at the composite. If the eyes look too strange just undo the Liquify filter and repeat with more subtle settings.

5   Once all is well flatten the image and save the file.

6   If you are still not satisfied, step back, select and delete Malc's left eye (the narrower one), duplicate his right eye and move into position.

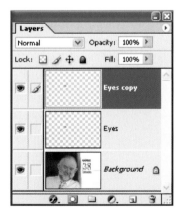

Backgrounds – Removal & Replacement

Photoshop provides many ways to remove backgrounds from images and even more ways to replace them. Here you will discover four methods of background removal. Along the way you will encounter a few other useful techniques. Towards the end of the project you will learn how to combine several images into a single file. This chapter is likely to take several hours to complete successfully.

Covers

Images on the website

Builder

Dress1

Dress2

Dress3

Salsun

One click removal

© Liberty of London

Only the simplest of backgrounds can be easily selected with the Magic Wand. This first section does, however, illustrate the principles involved and the fun you can have with changing backgrounds.

Magic Wand

1   As always Reset all Tools, and open the file Builder. Importantly the photograph has strong edges and a clean background which allows the use of this simple technique.

2   Duplicate the Background layer and turn off the visibility of the original bottom layer. With the Magic Wand select all the white background around the image. You should see two sets of "marching ants". Press the delete or backspace key to remove the unwanted background. Instant success! Deselect and save the file.

Don't forget the white areas around the shoulders.

Gray & white squares indicate transparency

Rename layers for better understanding.

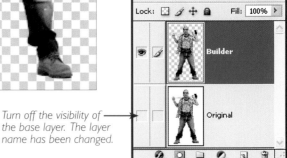

Turn off the visibility of the base layer. The layer name has been changed.

Simple background or tiled?

Always duplicate the Background layer when working on any image. This allows you to look at or return to the original very easily. Name layers to avoid confusion.

Make a new layer and color with a gradient. Don't be alarmed by the result. Solve any problem by changing the layer order.

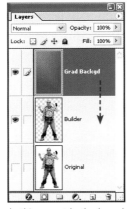 

In this example the layer has been colored with the Radial Gradient Tool. Drag to reposition in the layer stack.

The big advantage of keeping cutouts on their own layers is the flexibility of movement, duplication etc.

You may be perfectly happy with the simple graded background but it is easy to make it look as though the builder is working in a tiled bathroom or kitchen.

Make a new layer, name it "Floor". Make a rectangular selection of the bottom third of the layer and fill with color and gentle texture. The example used Filter > Noise > Add Noise. Deselect.

Never paint on the cutout layer. Create new layers for all new items.

Make sure the Floor layer is beneath the Builder layer

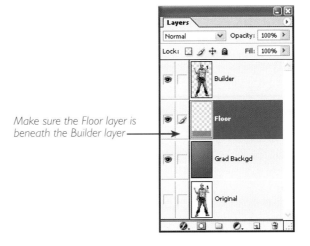

4 Add a pattern. The example shown used Filter > Texture > Tiles. The settings used are shown below.

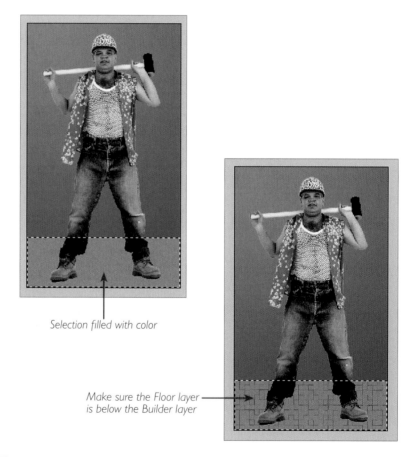

Selection filled with color

Make sure the Floor layer is below the Builder layer

5 Distort this tiled layer to create the floor using Edit > Transform > Distort.

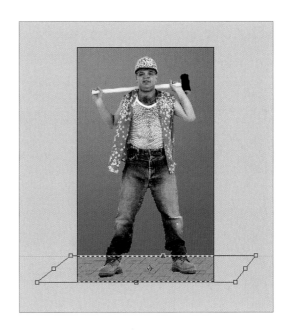

6 Make a new layer and call it "Wall".
Position this layer beneath the Floor layer in the layer stack.

7 Add a gradient, and optionally Filter > Noise > Add Noise.

8 Follow this with Filter > Texture > Mosaic Tiles.
Lastly Select > Deselect.

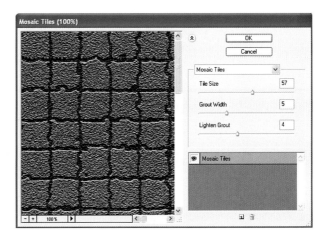

9 For added impact you may want to add a drop shadow as described on page 154. The end result is shown below. Decide if you want to flatten the image or not and save the file.

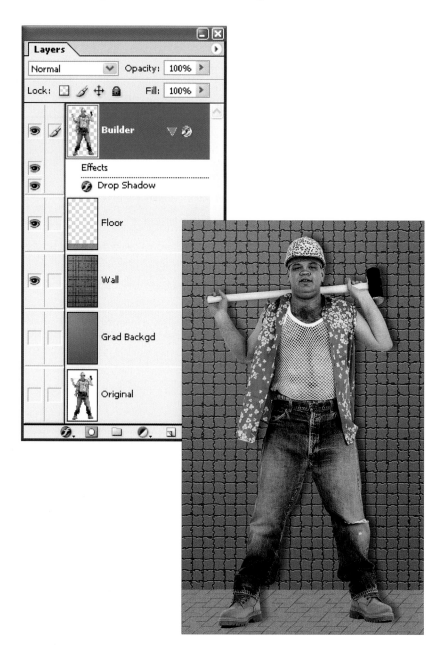

Eraser Tools

© John Slater

For the next part of this project you will compare two different methods of background removal using similar subjects. Evaluate which technique is best for your own images. Often you will need more than one tool to successfully complete a single task. Here you will use a combination of Eraser Tools to remove the backdrop to an image shot in a studio.

1 Open the file Dress1 and make any color and tonal changes you think necessary.

2 Pick the Background Eraser Tool and set the options similar to those shown below.

Use the Eyedropper to sample the subject and so change the foreground color. This color will be protected from removal.

3 Start at the left elbow and work upwards keeping the hot spot of the cursor just outside the line of the model. Work your way around the figure changing the Protect Foreground Color. This is especially important at the bottom of the dress where the colors are very similar. It will be very difficult to get this right first time. Don't worry – there is a plan!

Keep the center of the cursor (the hot spot) outside the edge of the image, otherwise areas needed may be erased.

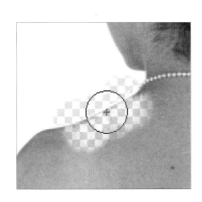

As soon as you start using the Background Eraser Tool the opaque Background Layer is converted into a conventional layer.

4 When you have been all around the image switch to the Magic Eraser  . Click on the excess background at the edges of the image to remove.

5 To reinstate areas accidentally removed pick the Eraser Tool and tick ☑ **Erase to History** in the Options bar. Paint over the areas needed.

6 Save the file as MyDress1.psd.

Use short mouse strokes. Each movement becomes an entry in the History palette – so it is easy to step back if you make a mistake.

Step 3

Step 4

Step 5

Extract

© John Slater

This image is slightly more difficult in that the hair is somewhat more whispy which may cause a problem. If you do lots of very fine background removal then special software is available – but perhaps Photoshop is all you will ever need!

Skill and understanding needed

If you are using a version of Photoshop prior to v6 Extract is not available. Use one of the other methods described.

1   Open the file Dress2 and make any color or tonal corrections you feel necessary.

2   From the Menu go Filters > Extract to reveal the Extract dialog shown below.

3   With the Edge Highlighter work around the image.
    This is shown here in green. Use the settings shown as a guide.

Edge Highlighter →

Fill Tool —

Eraser —

Cleanup Tool →

Edge Touchup Tool →

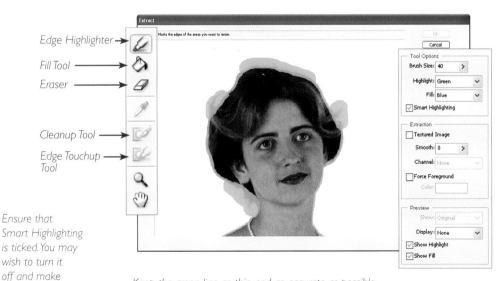

Ensure that Smart Highlighting is ticked. You may wish to turn it off and make the lines thicker where there is a difficult boundary such as the hair or the tassels at the bottom of Dress3.

Keep the green line as thin and as accurate as possible to ensure a good clean cut-out. Smart Highlighting makes the task much easier.

Using Extract will automatically convert an image into a Layer.

4 Use the Fill Tool to flood the interior of the image with color (shown here in blue). If the blue color appears all over the image there must be gaps in the green line. Zoom close and fix with the Edge Highlighter.

5 Click Preview to test your work. It may be good, but is it perfect? The likely answer is no. Which areas suffer essentially depends on your skill with the Highlighter Tool. In the example shown below the bottom of the dress is far from good. You may wish to change "Display" to Black or Gray to find the real extent of the damage!

If the Fill covers all of the image there is a break in the green line. Only the image should be colored as shown above.

It may be difficult to see imperfections in the extracted image on a transparent background. Try gray or black.

Refine

Refine any problem areas with the Cleanup and the Edge Touchup tools. Use the Cleanup Tool to add or remove pixels. If used at the default setting, this works like the Eraser and removes pixels. Press the Alt/Option key to reinstate areas that have been lost. The Edge Touchup sharpens the extracted boundary. The effect is cumulative with repeated use.

It is not immediately apparent how the Cleanup tool works – look to the top and bottom of the Extract dialog box.

Use the Edge Touchup Tool to clean up fuzzy edges.

The speed of the Cleanup Tool is controlled by pressing the number keys 1–9. Lower settings are recommended for more subtle results.

Use the Cleanup Tool to restore lost pixels or erase unwanted ones.

1　Where there are excess pixels remove them with the Cleanup Tool.

2　Where pixels have been lost reinstate them with the same tool but with the Alt/Option key pressed.

3　If you want to sharpen any boundaries use the Edge Touchup Tool.

4 Only when you are completely satisfied that you cannot improve the image further, press OK.

5 Save the file as MyDress2.psd. You will need it later.

6 Because Extract is such an important tool use it again to isolate Dress 3. Save this file as MyDress3.psd.

Dress 3

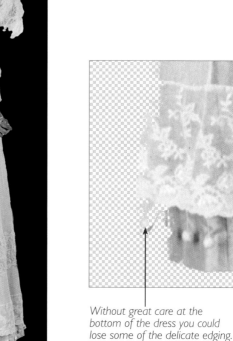

© John Slater

Do NOT flatten these images or you will lose the transparency.

The extracted Dress3 image shown against a black matte.

Without great care at the bottom of the dress you could lose some of the delicate edging.

Putting it all together

One of the most useful and important tasks is to combine several images into a single file. Use the extracted files to make a montage of three images.

1 Make a new file (File > New) to receive these images – either Letter or A4 size. Using the settings below you will end up with a white sheet of paper. Fill this with a pale color to make it more interesting. Rotate this file to create a "landscape" page.

In early versions there are no preset sizes – simply enter in the required dimensions. Go Image > Rotate Canvas to get a landscape page.

2 Open one of the files you have just extracted.
The one shown here is MyDress2.

3 Go Windows > Arrange > Tile.
The two files appear side by side. With the Move Tool drag the extracted model onto the new colored file.

Depending upon the version you are using the Tile command can be Window > Tile, or Widow >Documents > Tile, or Window > Arrange > Tile.

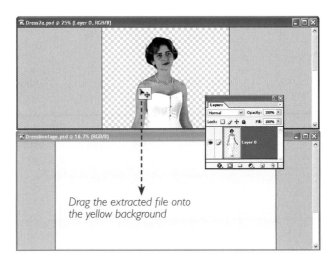

Drag the extracted file onto the yellow background

4 The action of dragging automatically creates a new layer, similar to the Copy – Paste command.

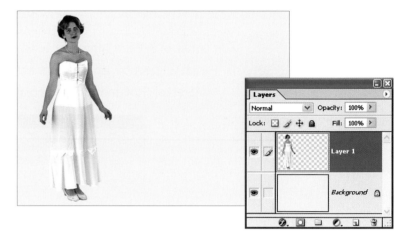

You can change the color of the background at any time.

5 Repeat for the other two extracted files. Save the file as Collage.psd.

6 In the Layers palette of this new file you should see a total of four layers.

Joined up writing – Paths

© John Slater

Remember long ago the perplexing step from printing to joined up writing? You may well experience similar difficulties with the Pen Tool which some people reckon is the most difficult tool to master. In Photoshop the Pen Tool is used to make Paths, which in turn are converted into selections. Paths are the professional way to make selections, particularly with objects that have smooth flowing lines and curves. You will gain a very basic introduction to pen techniques using an image from a furniture company. The image has two problems – part of the wood is of poor quality and the background is murky. Both will be solved with Paths.

Pen pal?

Don't let the look of this exercise put you off. The Pen is an important tool. Try drawing some shapes on a blank file before you get into a tangle.

Open the file Salsun. Pick the Pen Tool and ensure that the options are set as shown below.

If you have problems with this file, open the Layers palette and make sure you are working on the Background layer. If you see any colored dots, turn off the visibility of the Template layer.

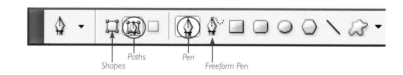

For this exercise ensure that the Pen Tools and Options are set as shown by the red circles

2. First something very easy. Replace the dark textured wood on the left of the tray with the good stuff on the right. Simply click on the four corners of the good piece of wood, shown as points A, B, C, and D on page 122. Complete the path by clicking back on the starting point A.

3 Open the Paths palette, Window > Paths to reveal the Work Path. Click on the palette arrow ▶ and Make Selection. You should see the customary "marching ants" around the piece of wood.

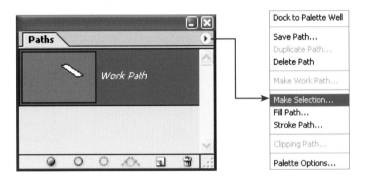

4 Put the selection on its own layer.
The clever way is Layer > New > Layer via Copy.

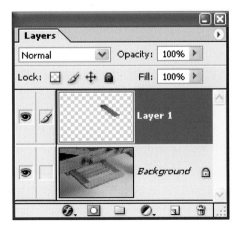

You discovered the distort commands in Chapter 5.

5 Reposition the new layer and use the distort commands to get the new wood exactly in position.

6 When exact, merge this layer with the Background layer. Click on the palette arrow  and choose Merge Down. Save as SalsunEND.tif.

Distort the new piece of wood to fit. You may find it easier to do this in stages.

This can be done with other selection tools but totally smooth lines are less likely.

Merge or flatten the layers ready for the next step.

Flowing lines

So far pretty simple. Now the tricky path to mastering smooth, curved selections begins.

Slightly more difficult is changing the background. The task is not that bad because most of the points are straight lines – identical to the previous task. Use the file Salsun2.psd which is similar to the file you have just made except that in the Layers palette there is a template to help with the next part of this project.

Turn on the visibility of the Template layer.

○ *Click on the yellow dots to create a straight line path.*

● *Click on the center of the red dots and drag to the center of the blue dots to create curved paths.*

● *Do NOT click on the purple dots – they are guidance points only.*

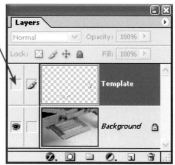

2   Pick the Pen Tool and join up the first five yellow dots.
Click on the first red dot, hold down the mouse and drag to the
next purple dot. Release the mouse. Nothing appears to have
happened but you *have* determined a direction for the path the
next time you click.

3   Click on the next red dot and drag to the following purple one.
The path should have curved around the corner. See how
adjusting the length of the line you drag affects the shape.

4   Continue the process until you return to the start point. Do not
forget the two yellow dots in the bottom corners.

Path Terminology

Before proceeding it is useful to understand the words used to describe the various parts of a path.

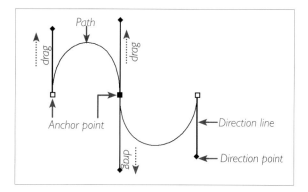

Refine

1 Zoom close and check the path. The chances are that you have not been totally accurate. You may wish to turn off the visibility of the Template layer. In the example shown below the straight lines of the path are not very good but can be easily adjusted with the Direct Selection Tool.

If the whole path moves you are using the wrong tool.

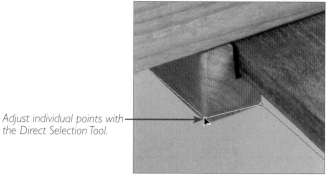

Adjust individual points with the Direct Selection Tool.

2 Check all other straight lines before proceeding.

3 Zoom into the first corner and with the Direct Selection Tool click on the path. You will see all the components of the path as shown at the top of the page.

4 If necessary, click on and move anchor points to alter the *position* of the path. Click and drag on the handles to alter the *shape* of the path. You should be able to make the path perfectly accurate. Repeat for the other corner.

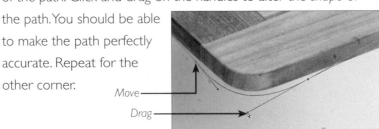

Move

Drag

5 From the completed path make a selection. Click on the palette arrow and "Make Selection". You are now free to change the background. Here a Gradient Adjustment layer was added and filled with tones ranging from white to mid gray. Note that in the Layers palette a mask appears in the shape of the selection.

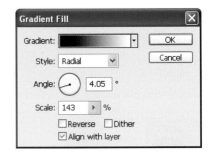

6 As a final touch make another small path in the triangular shadow area (top left) and add a Levels adjustment layer to lighten this section. Save the file.

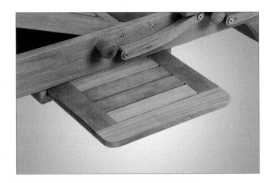

Drape

There are specialized programs and add-ons for Photoshop that allow you to seamlessly change clothing, fabrics and textures. Unfortunately these are very expensive. Here are a couple of ways to use Photoshop to achieve similar results. You will encounter two different types of "mask", both easily controlled with simple painting tools.

Covers

What you will achieve in this project

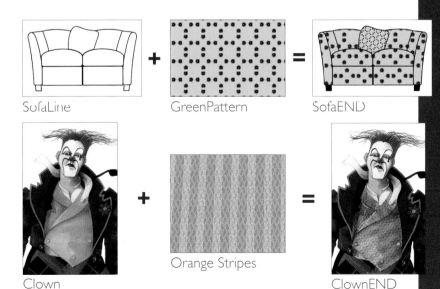

SofaLine   GreenPattern   SofaEND

Clown   Orange Stripes   ClownEND

Chapter Eight

Upholstery Assistant

It is clearer to understand complex techniques with simple illustrations. You are going to put "fabric" into a line drawing of a sofa and make it look realistic. You will use a pre-made pattern but if you wish, make your own as described on page 216.

Sew it all together

1 Open the file Sofaline and select the bottom two panels with the Magic Wand.

Use the SHIFT key to add to a selection.

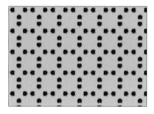

2 Open the GreenPattern file. From the Menu go Select > All. A set of "marching ants", a selection, appears around the edge of the file.

When you copy an image it goes to computer memory. It will stay there until you either copy something else or turn off the computer.

3 Then Edit > Copy. Close the file as it is no longer needed.

4 The Sofaline file and its selection should now be visible. Go Edit > Paste Into (NOT Paste). The pattern fills the selected shape.

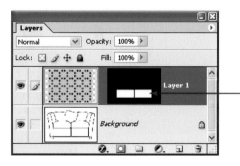

In the Layers palette notice masks appear – you will use exactly the same process to replace skies in a later chapter.

5 Use the Move Tool ⊹ to reposition the pattern.
Try and get the pattern symmetrical.

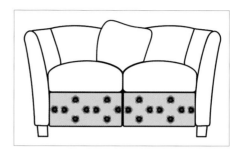

If you get this happening, you are on the wrong layer.

6 Repeat for all other sections of the sofa and the cushion. Alter the scale of the pattern in the cushion (Edit > Transform). Save the file as SofaEND.

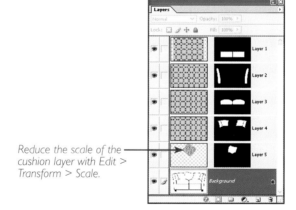

Reduce the scale of the cushion layer with Edit > Transform > Scale.

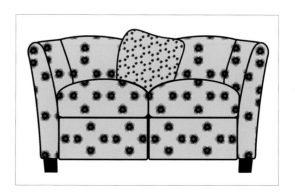

Draper's Assistant

© David Collis

You are going to create a drape effect for a new fabric. This is best done if the original, or the selection, is not patterned and is also monochrome. In the example shown you will isolate the waistcoat from the rest of the image using a technique known as Quick Mask and add another image in sections to create a sense of depth to the clothing. The process has lots of steps, but in reality is very simple.

Make the selection

1 Open the file Clown and make a very rough selection of the waistcoat with the Lasso or the Magic Wand. It does not matter that the selection is imperfect.

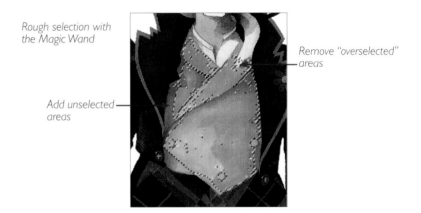

Rough selection with the Magic Wand

Remove "overselected" areas

Add unselected areas

2 Double-Click on the Quick Mask button at the bottom of the Toolbox. Set the Options as shown below.

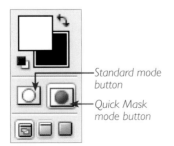

Standard mode button

Quick Mask mode button

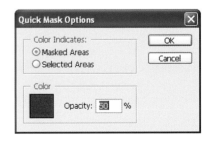

3 The mask can be changed by any of the Painting Tools. Paint with black to add to the mask and paint with white to remove the mask. Gray will add translucency and softness, similar to feathering.

Constantly swop between Standard & Quick Mask Mode to check the selection.

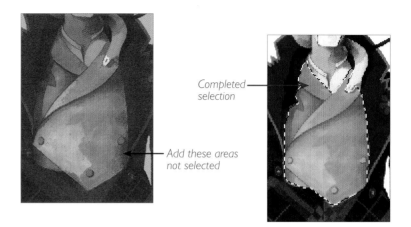

Completed selection

Add these areas not selected

4 When the Quick Mask is complete revert to Standard mode to see the selection. Copy the waistcoat onto its own layer. Try Layer > New > Layer via Copy.

5 Unless you want to change the color of the new fabric/pattern, make sure the waistcoat has no color. Use Image > Adjust > Desaturate.

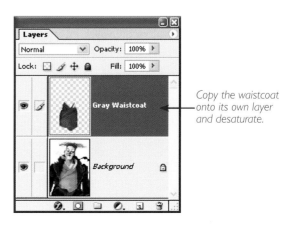

Copy the waistcoat onto its own layer and desaturate.

Layer Sets

The new gray waistcoat layer is too dark. This can be easily remedied with a Levels adjustment. To retain flexibility use an adjustment layer. To have this only affect the gray waistcoat make a Layer set of the Waistcoat and its adjustment layer.

1 Open the Layers palette and click on the New set button at the base of the palette. Change the name and options as you wish. Here the set is yellow.

Level Sets have only been available since version 6.

2 Drag the Gray Waistcoat layer into the Set.
The folder icon will open when you are in the right place.

3 Click the adjustment layer button and choose Levels. This has the same effect as the normal Levels command. Adjust as shown.

4 Change the SET blending mode to Normal and notice that the changes now only affect the waistcoat.

If the set mode is not changed, all the image will be affected by the change.

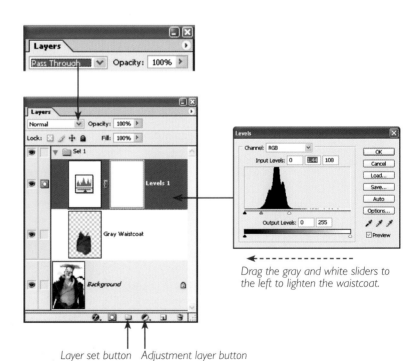

Drag the gray and white sliders to the left to lighten the waistcoat.

Layer set button   Adjustment layer button

Create the Drape

To increase realism add the new fabric in sections and transform each section. Use Quick Mask to make selections.

When you copy anything it will stay in memory of the computer until something else is copied or you turn off.

1 Open the file OrangeStripes. Select > All of the image and copy with Edit > Copy. Close the OrangeStripes file as it is no longer needed.

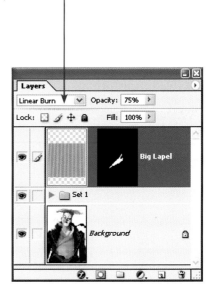

After making the selection close the Layer set. New layers will appear above the set and not in it.

2 Use the Lasso, Magic Wand and/or Quick Mask, to create a selection of the lapel of the waistcoat.

3 Now the moment of truth. Edit > Paste Into.
The Orange fabric is pasted into the shape of the lapel. Look at the Layers palette and see that the fabric is on its own layer and a mask has been created. For added realism change the blending mode. Suggestions are Multiply and Linear Burn.

Do NOT choose PASTE.

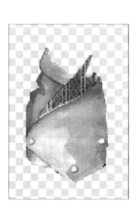

4 Pick the Move Tool and reposition the fabric (spooky). In addition you can scale and rotate using the Transform and Free Transform commands Edit > Transform / Free Transform.

When using the Transform commands zoom out so that you can see all of the transform box.

Move to the gray waistcoat layer to make additional selections.

5 Repeat for the other parts of the waistcoat. If you find that you have "cracks" between adjacent areas of cloth, you can easily fix them by painting in the Mask of the layer in question.

If your selections are less than perfect some of the underlying gray waistcoat will be seen ——

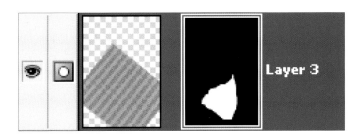

The mask can be painted with black or white paint to reveal more or less of the layer below. Click on the mask first to reveal the mask icon. Paint on the image with black or white paint.

6 Once you are sure that all the pieces of the pattern are exactly the way you want them, and there aren't any cracks, turn off the visibility of the Background layer and Merge Visible to simplify the Layers palette.

If a layer is accidentally included in the layer set simply drag it to the top of the layer stack.

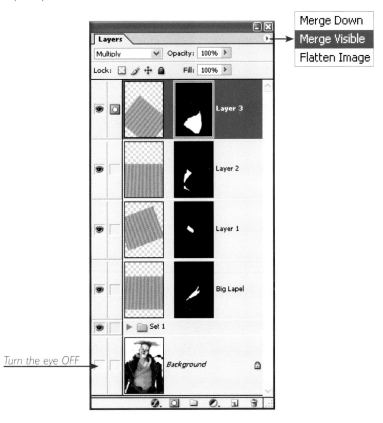

Turn the eye OFF

Finishing Touch

Enhance the drape effect by adding sheen or highlights to the cloth.

1 Make a new layer and name it "Highlights".

2 With white paint work around the image adding highlights where required. Change the blending mode to Screen and lower the opacity.

3 Flatten all layers and save the file as ClownEND.

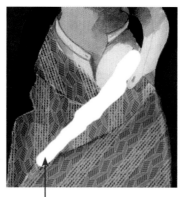

For the purpose of illustration paint is shown here at full strength. It would be better to apply with the Opacity at a much reduced strength.

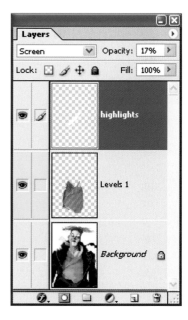

Panoramas & Skies

How many times have you been in a fantastic location only to find that your camera lens is either not wide enough or cannot convey the shear scale of the landscape? Taking a series of images and merging them into a panorama may be the answer. Additionally you will be shown how to replace a dull and uninteresting sky in an otherwise dramatic landscape. Your understanding of Layer masks will be stretched. In the latest version of Photoshop there is a photomerge feature that can be used to make panoramas – but it will not achieve the quality available with the manual techniques shown here.

Covers

Images to use and create

Emerald

Clouds

VolcanoEND

Chapter Nine

Panoramas

With modern cameras and ultra-wide angle lenses it is easy to capture large vistas. Inevitably this means that important subject matter remains in the distance. Shooting panoramas with normal or even telephoto lenses can increase the potency of your photographs. Although images are provided for you to use, this is a much more satisfying experience if you take the trouble and plan your own pictures. It is possible to do this without a tripod, as in the example described here, but it does make the Photoshop work more difficult.

Shoot the pictures

1 Use a tripod even though it is difficult to get perfectly level.

Buy a bubble from a camera store to help set the camera level. Set the camera exposure manually so that each shot is exposed exactly the same. If left on Automatic there will inevitably be variation, especially in the sky.

2 Select a lens and do a trial run. Watch the horizon to see if it changes position in the viewfinder. Allow 25% to 40% overlap between shots – bigger overlap will usually provide easier and better alignment when the images are put into Photoshop.

3 Think about shooting with the camera in "Portrait" mode.

Minimum Overlap

Optimum Overlap

© John Slater

Assembly

The files provided are Volcano1, Volcano2, Volcano3 and Volcano4. Open Volcano1 – this is the left edge of the finished picture. Create extra space to the right to accommodate the other three images. Increase the canvas as shown below using Image > Canvas Size.

Use "percent" in the Canvas Size box and avoid the difficult maths.

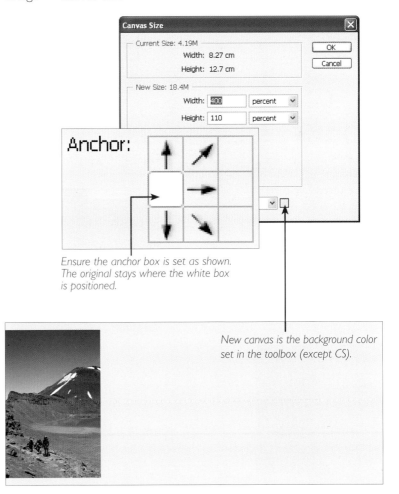

Ensure the anchor box is set as shown. The original stays where the white box is positioned.

New canvas is the background color set in the toolbox (except CS).

Use the arrow keys to nudge layers and get better alignment.

Open Volcano2 and drag the image onto the enlarged Volcano1 with the Move Tool. Rename the new layer and align the two images as best you can. Close the Volcano2 file.

3 Make a layer mask for the Volcano2 layer.

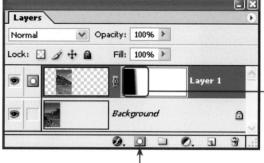

Click the default swatches button to get pure black and pure white.

Click here to create a Layer mask

4 Drag a black to white linear gradient across the overlap zone and an instant blend is achieved – the gradient is applied to the mask.

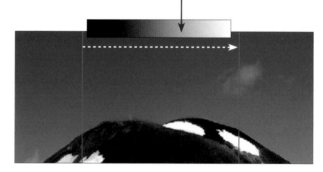

Turn off the visibility of the base layer to see how the gradient and mask are working together.

5 Your image should be looking pretty good. You may need to re-check your alignment if you see any ghost images. If this proves difficult, try rotating the top layer gently with Edit > Transform > Rotate. Misalignment is usually caused by not using a tripod.

Check for ghosting

6 Repeat the whole process for the files Volcano3 and Volcano4. The Layers palette should look something like this.

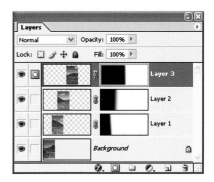

7 When you are totally convinced everything is in good order the layers can be flattened and the image cropped. Save the file as VolcanoEND.

Volcano 4 is much darker than the other sections. Make a Levels adjustment on this layer to balance the densities.

Tidy up with the Crop Tool

The section inside the dotted line shows approximately what you would see with a 24mm lens.

New skies for old

Sometimes you take a photograph in a fantastic location but poor weather makes the picture less exciting, less dramatic. This exercise shows you how to take a powerful sky from one image and seamlessly replace a dull and dreary sky in another. Be prepared for the WOW! factor. This exciting exercise revolves around the insignificant looking Paste Into command you experienced in the previous chapter. Do you get the idea that Paste Into is much more interesting and more useful than it first appears?

Organize the desktop

Open the file Emerald. Maximize the image area and open the Layers Palette. This consists of a single *Background* layer showing a thumbnail of the Emerald Lake landscape. Leave this palette open, but drag it to one side of the screen.

Depending upon the version of Photoshop, the tile command may be Window > Tile, Window > Documents > Tile, or Window > Arrange > Tile.

For some strange reason the Tile command was not available on the Mac before v7. Even in v7 the tiles appear horizontally on the Mac and vertically on the PC.

2 Without closing the Emerald file, open the file Clouds.
Although the next step is not strictly necessary it is good working practise. Go Window > Arrange >Tile.
The two images automatically move side by side.
It is also recommended that you position the Layers palette between the two images, as shown next.

...cont'd

Reset Tools to their default settings (page 20) before starting each exercise. This is particularly important in a shared environment such as college, where other users are likely to have changed some settings.

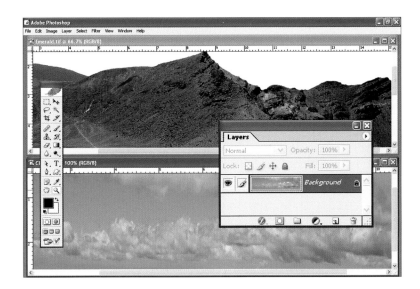

The Layers palette shows a thumbnail of the cloud file and because it is highlighted, it is the "active" file. Anything you now do will only affect this, the active image. You are going to enhance the Emerald landscape by putting the clouds inside a selection of the lifeless sky.

Stronger than Paste

Ensure that the Cloud file is active, then Select > All.
The marching ants should be running around the edge of the image. Then Edit > Copy.

When you use the Copy command, nothing visible happens but the image is copied to the memory of the computer. It will remain in memory until you either turn the computer off or copy something else.

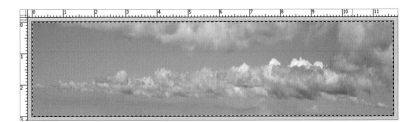

2 Close the Cloud file without saving any changes. Make the Emerald file active and with the Magic Wand set at the default tolerance of 32, click on the sky. The selection should follow the outline of the dull sky.

3 Now the fun bit. Go Edit > Paste Into (not Paste). The clouds are pasted into the area within the marching ants. To get this into your head, think "Paste into the selection" or "Paste into the shape". Even better ...... pick the Move Tool and move the clouds within the outlines of the sky.

Choose Paste Into, not Paste. If Paste Into is gray, you forgot to copy the clouds. If the clouds appear on top of the image, you selected Paste instead of the correct Paste Into.

Make a selection of the sky with the Magic wand.

Copy the clouds and Paste Into the selection. If necessary use the transform commands to adjust the size of the copied image.

To understand what has happened look at the Layers Palette. Layer 1 now consists of the clouds and a mask in the shape of the sky. You didn't have to make the mask, this happens automatically with the Paste Into command. You will continue to learn about masks in later chapters.

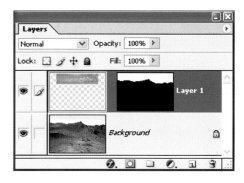

When the Paste Into command is used a new layer (Layer 1) is automatically created, plus a Layer mask in the shape of the selection – in this case the sky.

Expand your horizon

1 Before you congratulate yourself, take a close look at the boundary between the sky and the mountains. There is a very good chance you will see a white edge.

Zoom in and check for a white line at the sky boundary.

2 Step back in time with the History palette. Make the selection again but this time make the selection marginally bigger with Selection > Modify > Expand.

3 Choose the minimum setting shown below.

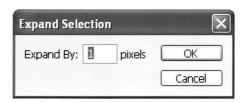

4 Paste Into again and this time there is no white edge. Save the file.

Name Layers

If you want to save your files with all layers intact, it is professional to name the layers, as explained below. If you need to put images into other applications, such as a Word document, it is necessary to flatten or merge all the layers together. You have a choice.

Whenever you see an interesting or dramatic sky, take a picture. This way you can build a collection of skies to use when needed.

Rename Layer1 as "Clouds". There are several ways to do this, here go Layer > Layer Properties.

Only flatten images when you are sure editing is complete. There is no easy way to go back. Flattened images occupy less disk space than layered images. For all the exercises in this book only three formats are needed: Photoshop PSD for layered files, TIF for normal flattened files and JPEG for compressed files.

Save the file as Emerald2.psd. This format keeps the layers intact and makes any future editing easy.

The final image should look something like this.

Brochure Project

You have already gained experience of blending layers and layer masks. The masks were created automatically – now you will take control. Smooth selections are generated from Paths. Paths are created with the Pen Tools. You are not expected to be an expert with these tools yet, so two pre-made paths are provided to assist the learning process.

Covers

Images for this project

Logo

Yacht

Watch

Brochure front cover

© Michel Herbelin

You are going to merge three images to create the front cover for a brochure. The background image is an ocean going yacht. The foreground image is a watch. The two are blended seamlessly. Additionally there is some type – a logo created in a drawing program. The watch photograph was taken in a studio and has several areas that need to be eliminated.

Ideal World

The two files you initially need for this project are Yacht and Watch. The Yacht file is the background for the collage. In an ideal world you would drag the watch onto the Yacht file and make a path with the Pen Tool of the areas you want to remove. Convert the paths into selections and delete – job done! It is unlikely that you are at this stage yet so you have a helping hand.

A basic guide to the Pen Tools can be found on page 121. If you get a shape instead of a path the options for the pen tool are set incorrectly. Delete the shape layer and start again.

Reality

Pen Tools are used to get smooth flowing lines. If you use other selection tools with this image the results will be less than perfect. To assist you two paths have already been drawn on the Watch file. Use or ignore these as you wish.

The Pen Tool is a very useful tool but requires skill that is only gained through practise and an understanding of the process.

1   Open the file Watch and open the Paths palette with Window > Paths. You will see two paths corresponding to the top and bottom edge of the Watch file.

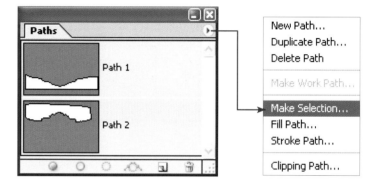

2   Make Path 1 active and it appears on the image. Zoom in to take a close look. Pick the Direct Selection Tool [↖] and click on the path. Adjust by moving the anchor and direction points. Undo any changes with the History palette.

Zoom in and take a look at the path. Move the anchor points and handles to help your understanding. Undo any changes afterwards.

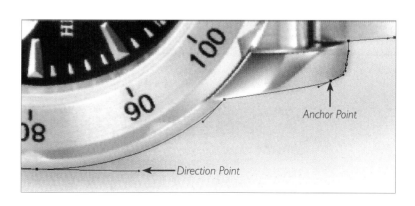

In the Make Selection box ensure that "New Selection" is checked.

3 Click on the palette arrow, choose Make Selection. The "marching ants" reveal one of the areas you want to delete, but before doing so open the Layers palette.

4 Change the *Background* layer to a conventional layer by double-clicking on it.

If you do not have a true layer you cannot delete to transparency.

Double-click on the Background layer to convert it into a true layer.

5 Press the delete or backspace key to remove the unwanted white areas. Notice how smooth the edges are.

6 Repeat the process for Path 2.
You should end up with something like the image below.

Areas deleted to transparency are indicated by the gray and white squares

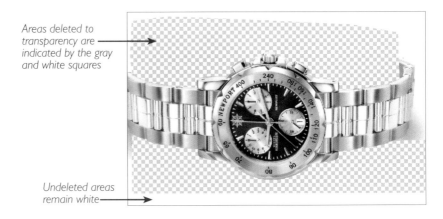

Undeleted areas remain white

Blend the images

First assemble the collage and then create interest by making the watch partially translucent, blending it with the sea.

You could have removed the unwanted white areas on the Watch file before dragging with either the eraser, or by altering the path before making the selection.

1 Open the Yacht file and drag the Watch on it with the Move Tool. Rotate and resize with Edit > Free Transform.

2 Remove the remaining unwanted white areas with the Eraser or the Lasso Tool.

Select remaining unwanted areas with the Lasso Tool and remove by pressing the delete or backspace key.

3 Use the shortcut button at the bottom of the Layers palette to create a Layer mask.

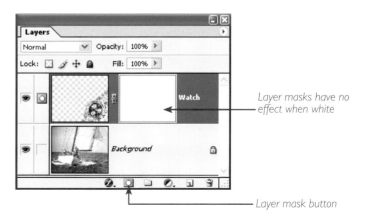

Layer masks have no effect when white

Layer mask button

...cont'd

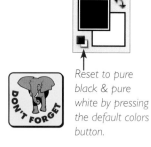

Reset to pure black & pure white by pressing the default colors button.

4 Set the foreground and background colors back to their default settings and the Brush Tool (Paintbrush) options similar to those shown below.

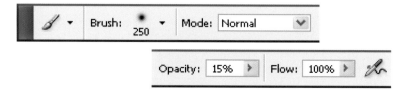

5 Start painting the bottom of the Watch strap and gradually see the strap become translucent. Change the Opacity to achieve a smooth blend.

Keep an eye on the Layer mask in the palette to help understand what is happening.

Paint with black to add transparency, gray for translucency and white to make opaque.

Add the Logo

© Michel Herbelin

Add the Logo using File > Place. The file is Logo.ai.

The file name Logo.ai indicates that the file originated in the drawing program Adobe Illustrator.

Drag the Logo by the corner handles to resize. Move to the top left. Press Enter/Return to accept the changes.

Hold down the Shift key to keep the perspective correct when resizing.

Change the text to white

In the Layers palette click on the lock transparency button. This does exactly what it says. Notice a padlock appears in the layer.

Lock transparent pixels button

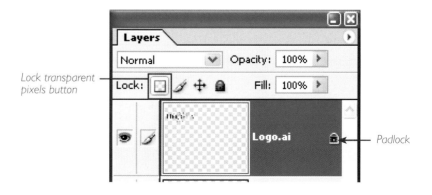

Padlock

2 From the menu go Edit > Fill > White. No selections are needed.

3 The white is not very effective by itself so enhance with a drop shadow using Layer > Layer Styles (Effects).

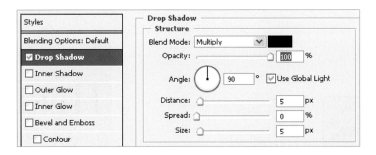

4 Keep the shadow subtle and note that the effect appears in the Layers palette. Save the file.

Alternative vision

Is there ever a perfect answer? Many designs can be changed to give a different feel and look. Here you will change the brochure and preserve the variations. Discover a few new tricks in the process, but you will need a keen eye as some of the changes are very subtle.

Use adjustment layers instead of menu commands to retain flexibility and avoid permanently changing the original.

Make a new Hue/Saturation adjustment layer and use the settings shown below. Blues are significantly reduced to leave an image that is essentially monotone with a few spots of orange wood on the boat.

Position the Hue/Saturation layer immediately above the Background layer so that it does not affect the watch.

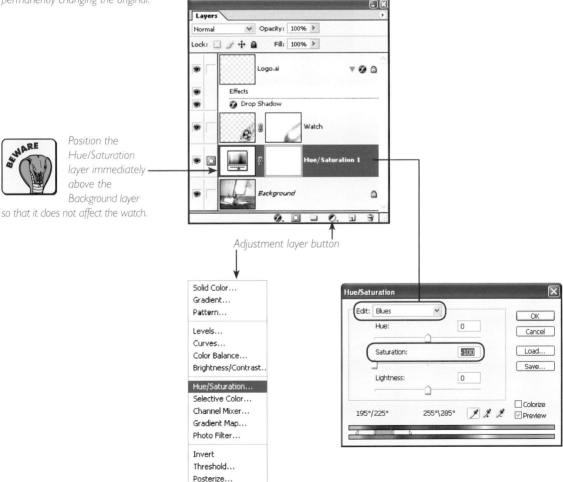

Adjustment layer button

This process essentially removes the blue cast from the sea and leaves the watch untouched. But what if you want the blue face of the watch to be richer in color?

2 Make another Hue/Saturation adjustment layer and position it above the watch in the Layer stack.

3 Pick "Yellows" and increase the saturation. Pick "Blues" and increase the Saturation. The watch, the yacht and the sea are all changed – possibly not what is required.

Some of the changes described here are very subtle.

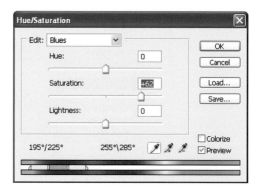

Layer sets 2

Layer sets first appeared in version 6.

In order to restrict the change to the watch a Layer set is needed. Layer sets have already been encountered on page 132.

1 Click on the Layer set button and create a new set. Identify the set with a red color.

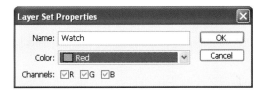

If the steel casing of the watch has a color cast eliminate with a subtle Layer mask.

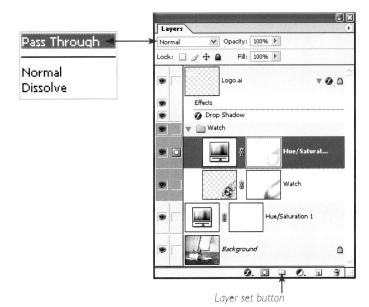

Layer set button

2 Drag the Watch layer and its Hue/Saturation layer into the folder icon of the new set.

3 Change the blending mode from "Pass Through" to "Normal". The increased saturation of blue and yellow now only affect the watch. Save the file.

Layer Comps

At this point you will have completed three versions of the brochure cover. Retain these within one document using Layer Comps – perfect for designers who want to show several alternative options to their clients.

Go Window > Layer Comps to show the Layer Comp palette. Click on the palette arrow, or the Create New Layer Comp button at the bottom of the Layer Comps palette. The new comp will be based on the current state of layers in the Layers palette.

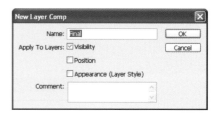

Layer Comps are not available in versions prior to CS.

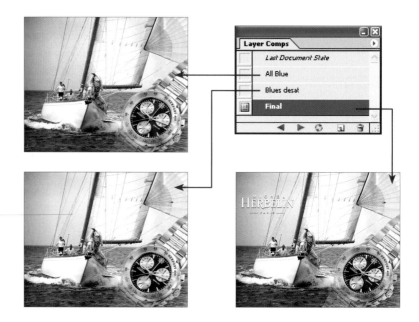

By default the number of entries in the History palette is 20. Increase this setting in the Preferences dialog box to at least 50.

Use the History palette to step back to the various intermediate points and generate the new Layer comps.

Type, Shapes & Gradients

Most of the images used in this book started life in a digital camera. A few were scanned from the film originals. In this chapter you will create the image yourself, completely from scratch! Combine type with the painting tools to design a new ticket for the Paris Metro. There are many facets to this project.

Covers

Use your skill to create this:

MetroParis

Paris Metro

This project combines some techniques used earlier in the book with some interesting new skills. The idea is to make a design for a new re-usable card to reflect the modern changes happening on the Paris Metro. The project advances your understanding of Layers, Type, Shapes, Gradients and the Brush Tool.

Reflective Words

1 Make a new file with the dimensions shown below. File > New.

Change the foreground color to red before starting to type.

2 Type the words "MetroParis". If you do not have the font shown here use a similar bold font, a similar point size and red color.

Type appears on its own layer and can easily be repositioned with the Move Tool.

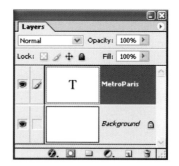

When you make the duplicate you will not see the new type until you move it.

3 Duplicate the Type Layer. Change the color of the copy to black, then flip (Edit > Transform > Flip Vertical) and move beneath the original text as shown below.

Change the names of layers to make them more understandable.

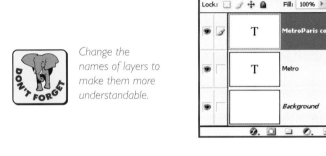

Realistic shadows

To make the shadow look more realistic the reflected type needs to fade towards its edges. This is achieved with a gradient.

If you see this sign you cannot proceed. Type layers are vector graphics and need to be rasterized into pixels before a gradient can be added.

Rasterize the reflected layer: Layer > Rasterize > Type. Notice the change in the Layers palette.

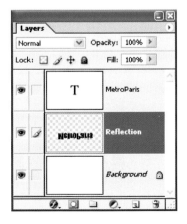

2 On the reflected layer select one letter with the Magic Wand. Select the rest of the text with Select > Similar and delete the black color by pressing the Delete or backspace key. Only the selection remains.

The black to transparent gradient will not work unless the contents of the selection are first deleted. You may want to turn off the visibility of the Background layer to see this happen.

3 Change the foreground color back to black.

4 Add a black to transparent gradient to the selection with the Linear Gradient Tool. When finished Select > Deselect.

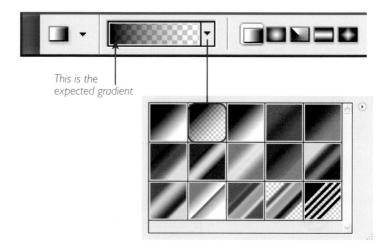

This is the expected gradient

The keyboard shortcut for deselect is Command/ Control + D.

Pick the Linear Gradient and drag in the direction shown to create the gradient.

Create Perspective

1 Distort the reflected layer until the type looks 3D as shown below. Use Edit > Transform > Distort.

Press the Return or Enter key to accept transform changes.

2 Rasterize the remaining type layer.

3 Link the two text layers together.

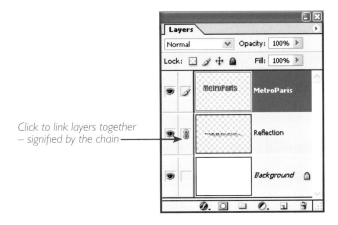

Click to link layers together – signified by the chain

4 Distort them to enhance the perspective.
Edit > Transform > Distort.

You may wish to unlink layers to fine tune the distortion.

Background detail

Give the *Background* a color and add a gradient effect. In the example shown the effect is a Radial gradient.

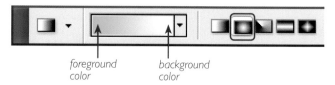

            foreground   *background*
            color   *color*

*Drag in this direction
to create the gradient.*

2 Add chevrons along the bottom of the image. You could draw a shape many times, but there is a better way. Pick the Custom Shape Tool and find the chevron shape. Draw a single shape in black. A new layer is automatically created.

If you cannot see the Chevron add it to the current shapes.

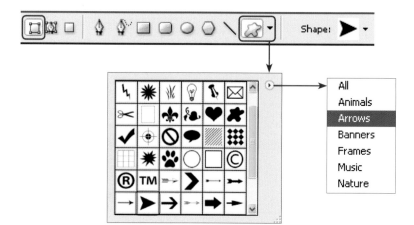

In older versions this is Edit > Define Brush.

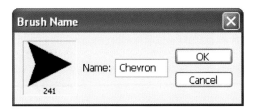

3 Turn the chevron shape into pixels with Layer > Rasterize > Shape, and temporarily turn off the visibility 🗙 of the *Background* layer.

4 Select the chevron with the Rectangular Marquee and Edit > Define > Brush preset. Give the new brush a name. Deselect and reinstate the visibility of the *Background* layer.

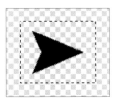

5 Click on the Brush Tool and open the Brushes palette 📄 Window > Brushes. Adjust your settings similar to those shown next.

Versions before CS do not have a "Flip" option. Use the Angle setting instead.

If you do not tun off the visibility of the Background layer the new brush will not be the simple chevron shape.

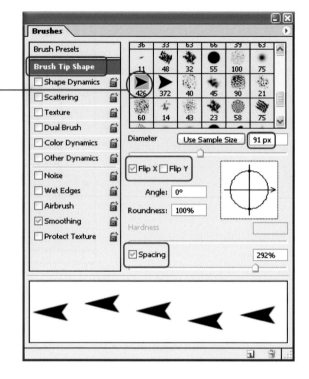

6   Make a new layer and call it "Chevrons". With the Paint Tool (Paintbrush) drag a line from extreme left to extreme right. Hold down the shift key for a perfect straight line.

Layer Styles and Layer Effects are the same thing.

7   Add text below the chevrons.

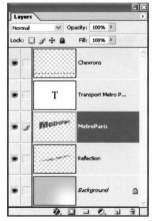

8 Move the original single chevron to the top left corner. Transform as necessary. Add some interest with a Layer Style. In this case go Layer > Layer Style > Bevel & Emboss. The settings used in the example are shown below.

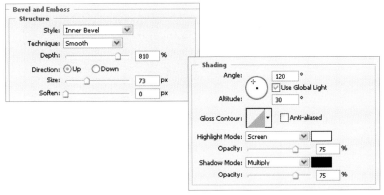

A little more flair

The card should be starting to look good. You have had to use lots of tools to get here. Now just a little flair to liven up the image.

1 Add dynamism with a shaft of white light running along the bottom of the text. Make a new layer and name it "Light Saber".

2 Pick the Reflected Gradient tool 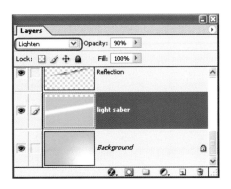 and choose white plus your background color as the gradient range. Draw the new gradient on the layer. It may take several frustrating attempts to get this right!

The Light Saber effect is on its own layer – so it can be moved. Make sure the Light Saber layer is positioned immediately above the Background layer in the stack and change the blending mode to Lighten.

3 Make the MetroParis layer active and add a bright highlight over the letter "O" using Filter > Render > Lens Flare.

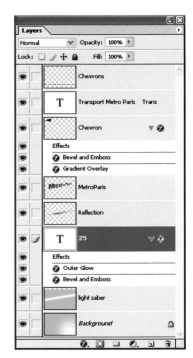

4 Experiment with the settings. Add some figures (25) and enhance using Outer Glow plus Bevel and Emboss in Layer > Layer Styles. Flatten the image and save the file as MetroParisEND.

Automate, Actions & Batch

Photoshop has many time-saving and productivity enhancing features. Besides being time efficient they are also fun to watch. In this chapter you will use four of the many options available. You should then have a clear idea of how all other Automate commands work. You will discover how to make a Contact Sheet, how to make a Web Photo Gallery and how to make repetitive tasks easy with Actions and Batch processing.

Covers

Images / software on the website

Orionjpg Folder   Digital Test Folder

LCFshoot Folder

BayHotel

Chapter Twelve

Contact Sheet

Batch...
PDF Presentation...
Create Droplet...

Conditional Mode Change...
Contact Sheet II...
Crop and Straighten Photos
Fit Image...
Multi-Page PDF to PSD...
Picture Package...
Web Photo Gallery...

Photomerge...

With the growth in the use of digital cameras everybody is taking more pictures. But how do you keep track of all these images? An image database is the perfect solution – but that's another piece of software to learn. A more traditional approach is to make a contact sheet. Conventionally this would be of a single roll of film but in Photoshop it can be any number of images. Importantly the images need to be assembled together in a folder before you start. A small collection of images are available for your use in the Orion JPG folder. These images form the basis of this project, but you should experiment with a larger number of your own images.

Organize and select the files

1 Collect all your images together and put them into a folder – or use the images in the Orion Folder which can be found on the website.

2 From the menu open the Contact Sheet dialog box with File > Automate > Contact Sheet. The box shown below appears.

The auto-spacing and rotate options usually make for a better design – but these are not available in versions prior to CS. Spacing can be changed manually by leaving the Flatten All Layers button unticked and then adjusting individual layers.

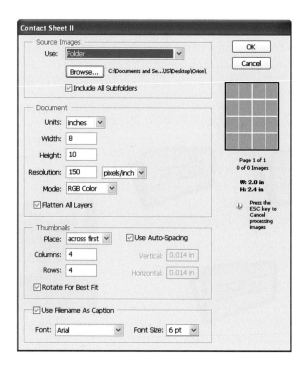

3 Choose the Source folder you want to use. In this example it is the Orion folder.

4 Set the size of the final contact sheet, the number of rows and columns, and click OK.

Typically you set the document size to your normal paper size. For a CD cover use the dimensions shown here.

5 Watch the show. Photoshop opens and reads each file in turn, makes a thumbnail and puts it into the contact sheet.

Thumbnails are generated on a layer so flatten the image before saving.

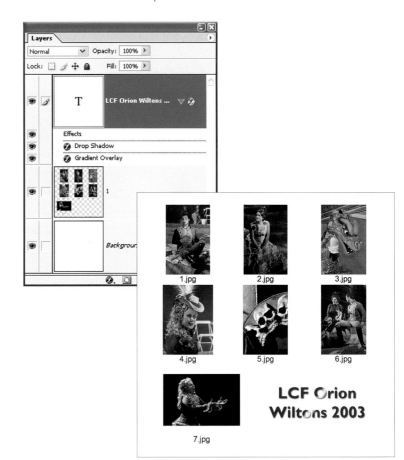

If you are making a CD of images include the contact sheet on the CD – i.e. make the contact before burning the CD.

6 When the process is finished add some descriptive text and, if required, Layer effects. Position the text and flatten the image. Save the Contact Sheet in the same folder as the images.

Web Photo Gallery

Many of the Automate commands are not available in Photoshop versions older than v6.

Photoshop will not replace web design programs such as GoLive, Dreamweaver or FrontPage, but will integrate with them. The great news is that Photoshop takes lots of the hard work out of creating web pages that are intended to display pictures.

Organize and select the files

1 Get started with File > Automate > Web Photo Gallery.

2 Pick a Style for the gallery from the Styles pop-up menu. You will need to experiment a little here to see what is available. The example shown uses the "Centered Frame 1 – Feedback" option.

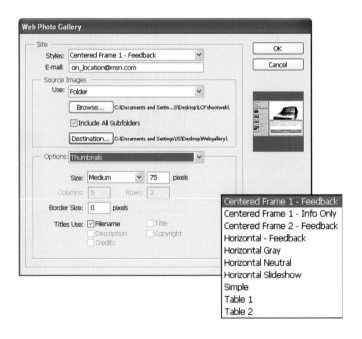

In Photoshop CS the templates from earlier versions can be found in the Goodies folder on the Install CD.

3 Customize web pages from the many options available.

4   The most important step is to choose the folder containing the images you want to use – the source folder. If your images are saved in different locations assemble these into a single folder. In the example shown the folder is called LCFshootweb, and this can be found on the website. This folder contains a selection of images from a theatrical costume photo shoot.

5   You must also choose or create a Destination folder, shown here as Webgallery.

6   Click OK and watch the show! Photoshop creates and places a large number of files in the destination folder. Check the results in a web browser before uploading to your site.

 The first or Home page created by most web design software is usually called index.html – just the same as one of the files generated by Photoshop. To avoid any possible conflict change the name of the Photoshop file.

View the finished web page – just click on the thumbnails to see enlarged versions of the images.

Actions

© John Slater

Actions are great for repetitive boring tasks. Simply record what you want to do to one image and then, with a single mouse click, apply the same changes to any other image. Here you will be shown how to use and modify one of the actions already supplied with Photoshop, how to create your own, and later how to apply an action to multiple images whilst you go and have a cup of tea!

Here's one I made earlier!

1 Photoshop is supplied with a good quantity and variety of pre-recorded Actions. Open the file BayHotel and go Window > Actions.

2 Expand the Default set and highlight Quadrant Colors as shown below. Expand this Action and press Play to watch the rapid show.

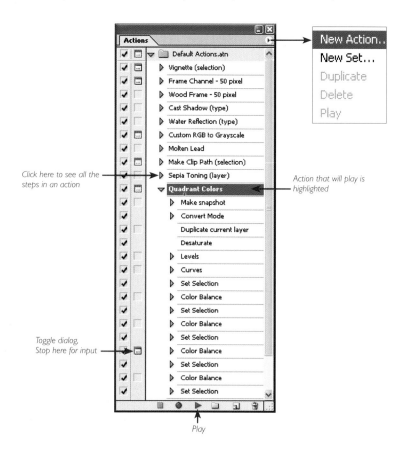

Stick your nose in

With some images you may wish to play only part of an action, or you may want to customize the prescribed settings.

1 Undo the last action with File > Revert.

2 Press the toggle button for the third occurrence of as shown on the previous page.

3 Run the action again but this time, at the point indicated, the process will pause and the Color Balance dialog appears. Input any settings you desire and press OK. The process continues until the end.

For ultimate control open the History palette and watch the progress of the Action. Noting and understanding these steps will allow you to easily develop your own Actions. You can go back to any point and adjust as you wish.

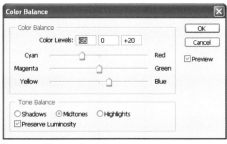

Pause the action to apply specific settings

4 Save the file.

Actions can be saved, copied and sent to friends.

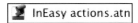

BayHotel file with the Quadrant Colors action applied

Make your own

Shown here are the steps needed to record an action. This action simply changes the resolution of an image from 72ppi to 300ppi – a very boring process when you have to do it to hundreds of images. This is typically what you need to do with images taken on some digital cameras to allow printing at photographic quality.

If you want to save files in different locations double-click on the "Save" step. This brings up the Save dialog and navigate to the new location. The settings are updated in the action.

1 Open the file BluFlowers (in the Digital Test folder) and open the Actions palette, Window > Actions. Click on the palette arrow ▶ and name the new action. Apply other settings if desired. From this point everything you do is recorded as a step in the Actions palette.

2 Open the Image Size dialog and ensure the Resample Image box is NOT ticked. Change the Resolution to 300 pixels/inch.

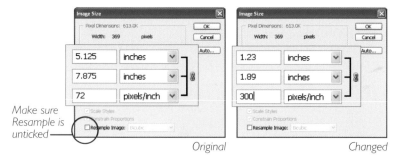

Make sure Resample is unticked

Original   Changed

3 Save the file and Stop the action. Try it out on other 72ppi images.

To test the action on another image click here and then the play button

If you want to change where images are saved just double-click here and enter a new location

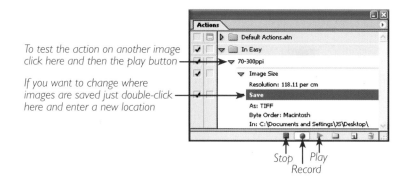

Stop Play
Record

Batch

The Batch command lets you play an action on any number of images within a folder. Batch eliminates the tedious processes involved when handling large numbers of similar files. Just imagine you could print a whole folder of images whilst you were out to lunch! You will actually process a number of images from a digital camera and change the resolution from 72 to 300ppi for printing, using the Action you have just created. Use your own images if you have them otherwise use the folder Digital Test Images.

Batch can be applied to pre-selected images in the Browser.

I   Assemble all the images you want to process into a single folder.

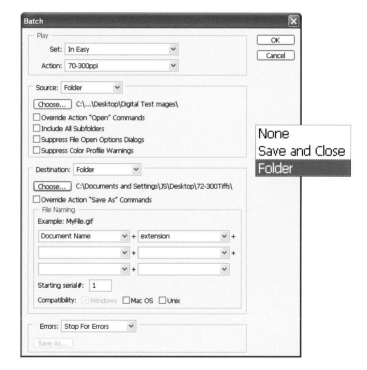

If you don't make a destination folder Save and Close will overwrite the original files. Selecting None will leave the files open for additional interaction from yourself.

2   Make a Destination folder for the processed images.

3   Choose File > Automate > Batch. You may not notice much has happened, but check the Image Size details and confirm that changes have occurred.

Slide show presentation

With each new release of the program Adobe are continually expanding the range of Automate features. New in version CS is a presentation feature which acts as a slide show and adds interest when viewing your images.

1 Start with File > Automate > PDF Presentation.

2 Either choose a folder of images (try LCFshootweb) or you can select individual images from any folder. Set any options required.

If your version of photoshop does not have this option you can still see the end result by downloading the file LCFshoot.pdf from the website.

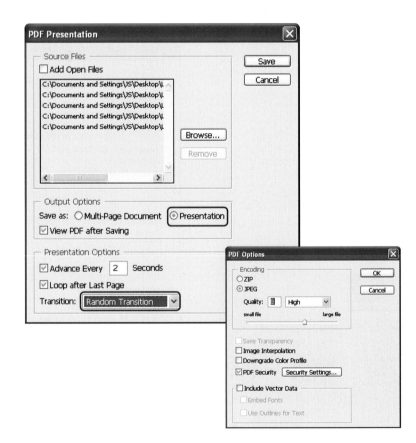

3 Click the Save button and any PDF options.

4 View the presentation with Acrobat Reader.

Cheat at Illustration

We are not born equal. Some of us can sing others just croak. Some of us can dance others have "wooden" legs. Some of us are naturally skilled illustrators whilst others are good photographers. No matter what your creative skills Photoshop gives you lots of opportunities to experiment with your ideas. Here are a few cheats!

Covers

Images you will create

Popgear

Seagulls

FashionShow

Alice

Shanghai

Chapter Thirteen

Andy Warhol fans look carefully

Whilst many photographers strive to extend the tonal range of their images, graphic designers have often found that reducing the number of tones can add impact to many images. In the 60's and 70's there was a tremendous explosion in the process of silk screening to produce images that were entirely dependant upon their graphic strength. One of the principal exponents of this technique was Andy Warhol. The following technique shows you how to reduce the number of tones in an image to just two, and then color them in. The project then involves making a piece of art fashioned after AW.

Reduce to B&W

For both the Posterize and Threshold techniques shown here you can use adjustment layers or Image > Adjustments etc. from the menu. Adjustment layers need to be flattened before making selections.

© John Slater

1 Open the file Shanghai.
   This is a continuous tone image taken with a digital camera.

2 Crop 🔲 the image roughly in half to concentrate just on the face.

3 Reduce the image to just black and white using the Threshold command, Image > Adjustments > Threshold.
   Adjust the slider similar to the diagram shown below.

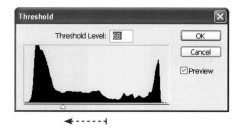

Add Color

Make selections with the Magic Wand and fill with solid color. This is not quite as easy as it looks, the numerous patches of white in the hair being a problem. A clever selection strategy is needed.

Selections can be easily adjusted with the Lasso Tool. Press and hold the shift key to add to a selection. Press and hold the Alt or Option key to remove from a selection.

1. With the Magic Wand select any white area and then Select > Similar. All white areas are selected.

2. With the Lasso Tool  set to remove from a selection, draw a loose shape around the face as shown below left. This will split the white selection in two. Fill the remaining selected area with bold color as shown below right.

If necessary move the mouse outside the picture window →

From version 6 onwards there are buttons in the Options bar that offer the same function as the Shift and Alt keys.

3. Select the remaining white area with the Magic Wand and the Select > Similar command. Fill with a complimentary color.

Add Remove

Ensure that the very small areas in the hair contain solid color —

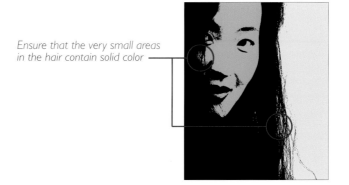

Now the art!

Make an image fashioned after Andy Warhol. Note that this project will allow three versions of the Shanghai image to comfortably fit on a Letter or A4 page in landscape mode. If you want more images than this you need to plan and adjust the size of the image now!

Image > Image size.

1 Duplicate the *Background* layer twice. The copies are stacked above the original and cannot yet be seen in the original.

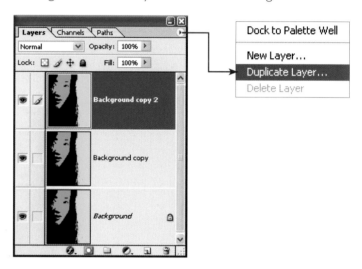

Use "percent" and avoid difficult arithmetic.

2 In order to move and see the duplicated layers increase the Canvas size – only the width needs increasing in this project.

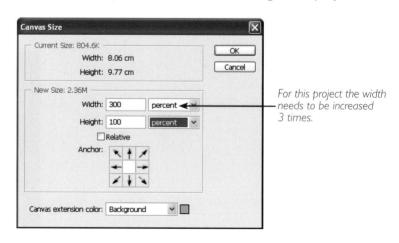

The increased canvas is the Background color in all versions of Photoshop except the latest CS which allows you to choose the color.

For this project the width needs to be increased 3 times.

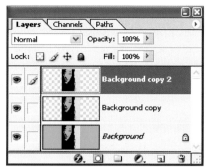

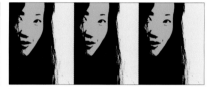

Increased canvas.

Increased canvas with images moved.

3 Move the copied layers to the left and right of the original with the Move Tool  as shown above right.

4 Select and color the duplicated images using the Magic Wand and the Select > Similar command.

5 Flatten the layers and save the file as ShanghaiEND.

Reduce tones with Posterize

© John Slater

Posterization reduces the tonal range of an image – to a specified amount. For example, choosing two tonal levels in an RGB image gives six colors, two for red, two for green, and two for blue. Pictures to benefit best from this technique should not be too highly detailed – lines and shapes are best.

1 Open the file Seagulls and crop as shown below.

2 Go Image > Adjustments > Posterize and set the levels to 4. Look carefully and you will see that there are twelve colors, four for each of the three channels. These colors can be changed using the selection techniques shown earlier in this chapter.

RGB images have three channels: Red, Green and Blue.

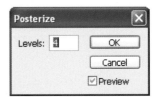

3 Tidy up the image with the Clone Stamp and Brush Tool. In the example shown part of a wing was removed and the people repositioned. Save the file.

More Color Control

© John Slater

Posterize effects can have a particularly strong influence on grayscale and monotone images.

1 Open the file Alice. This image has already been cropped into a panoramic format to add impact. You might like to enhance the image by cloning out the fence post in the background.

2 Turn this into a grayscale image using Image > Adjustments > Desaturate.

Use adjustment layers instead of menu commands when you want to retain the flexibility to adjust any changes.

3 Make a Posterize adjustment layer (page 70).
Choose the number of levels you feel appropriate.

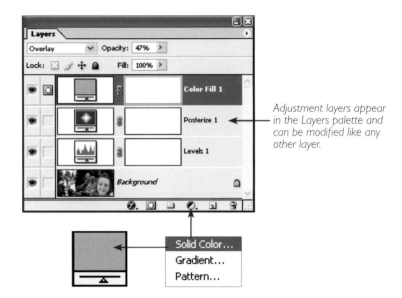

Adjustment layers appear in the Layers palette and can be modified like any other layer.

4 Add a single hue to all the tones using a solid color Adjustment layer. Don't worry that the image goes blank – just alter the Layer blending mode. Suggestions are Overlay and Color. Reduce the Opacity if you like.

5 Flatten the image and save as AliceEND.

Ultimate Color Control

© John Slater

Imagine you want to use the image PopGear in a poster celebrating British pop music of the 60's and 70's. The idea is to break down the image into a series of tones and color these red, white and blue – the colors of the flag. In the traditional darkroom technique for posterization, negatives were made for each tone or color required. You will do just the same but it will be much quicker and very much easier.

1 Open the file Popgear and desaturate to make it appear grayscale using Image > Adjustments > Desaturate.

2 Posterize the image to 4 levels using the menu commands. Don't worry about the spotty areas on the shoulder and neck – these can be removed later if necessary.

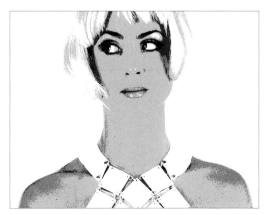

...cont'd

Fuzziness controls the degree to which related colors are included in the selection. It will not greatly affect this image unless extreme values are set. In this project it is essentially used to select similar colors throughout the image.

Paint or erase "spotty" areas to tidy up the graphic.

Make selections from the Background layer.

3 Open the Color Range dialog (Select > Color Range) and with the first eyedropper click on the gray on the neck. Set the Fuzziness control to the value shown. Click OK and end up with a selection.

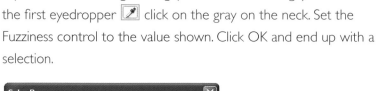

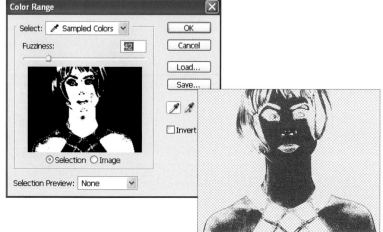

4 Make a new layer and fill the selection with red. Deselect.

5 Repeat the whole process for all the white areas and fill the selection with blue. Deselect.

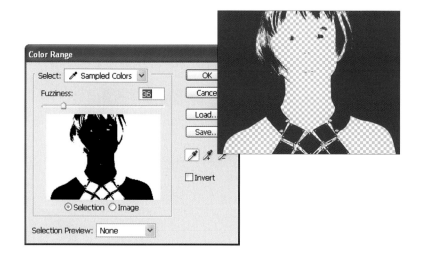

6 Make a new layer and fill with white. Position the layer just above the grayscale original in the layer stack. The Layers palette should look like this:

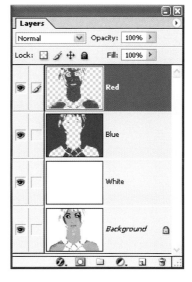

Instead of using Color Range you could use the Magic Wand and the Select > Similar command. Unfortunately this creates two tones and not the single color desired. Try this and see the effect at the edges of the hair.

7 Turn off/on the visibility of the White layer as you see fit. Save the file as BritEND.

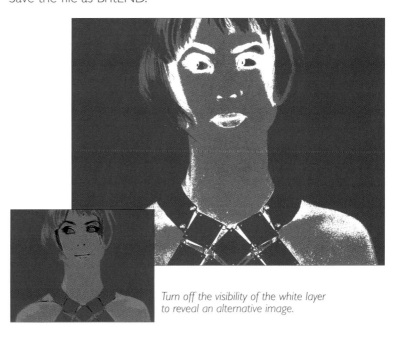

Turn off the visibility of the white layer to reveal an alternative image.

Draw to History

© John Slater

There are several techniques that allow photographs to be transformed into line drawings. You can then combine the line drawings with any intermediate step – a fascinating and endless opportunity for creative exploration.

Open the file FashionShow and apply Smart Blur.
From the menu go Filter > Blur > Smart Blur.

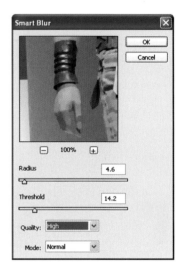

Experiment with the Radius and Threshold settings to get more or less detail.

Smart Blur is not essential but it will reduce significantly the number of fine lines and this is likely to be beneficial to the end result.

2 Then Filter > Stylize > Find Edges.
This gives an image with colored lines.

3 Remove the color with Image > Adjustments > Desaturate, and enhance with a Levels adjustment.

The more the white slider is moved to the left the more fine detail is removed – this may be what you want.

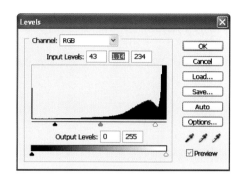

Make sure you pick the History Brush and not the Art History Brush.

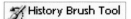
History Brush Tool

4 Now the fun really begins. Pick the History Brush in the Toolbox and set the options as shown below.

5 Open the History
palette (Window >
History) and click in
the space next to the
Smart Blur entry. This is
the History state you
will paint back to.

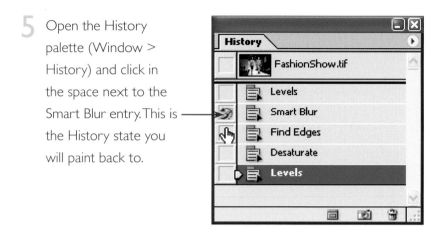

6 Start painting over the line drawing and like magic the color starts
to reappear. If you are using the settings given repeated painting
will add to the density.

7 Save the completed image as FashionShowEND.

Picture Framer

When you have finished your masterpieces they deserve to be framed and displayed. This chapter shows you how to enhance pictures with keylines, mattes and frames created on the computer. Your skills with the selection tools will be tested.

Covers

Images on the website

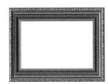

Frame

VolcanoEND

Liberty

Lion

PaintingEND

Flowers

Chapter Fourteen

Keyline and Background Color

© John Slater

In the real world images are enhanced and improved by lines, borders and frames. Why not do the same with your digital images "before" you print them? You could even use this technique to check out what works with your images before sending them off to the picture framer.

Always use print with Preview

Print Preview is called Print options in v6 and was not available in earlier versions.

1 Open the file LibertyEND and crop as shown left.

2 When you print any file it is strongly recommended you do this via Print Preview. Go File > Print with Preview.

There are many options. One of the most elegant is a simple keyline around the image – especially powerful if lots of white space remains. Click on [Border...] and enter the desired line width. The line will be black.

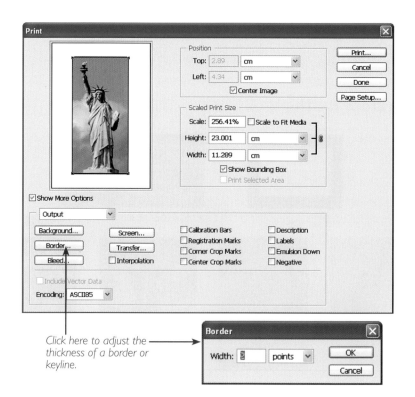

Click here to adjust the thickness of a border or keyline.

3 Untick ☑Center Image but make sure the Show Bounding Box is ticked. Reposition and, if desired, scale the image. The end result will be an image on a white background with a narrow subtle border.

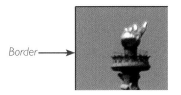

Border —————→

4 When pictures are framed for real a card matte is often put over the artwork for protection and enhancement. A simple way to simulate this is to add a background color when printing. Click on the Background button Background... and choose the desired color. In truth you may find this technique not very elegant – a better alternative follows.

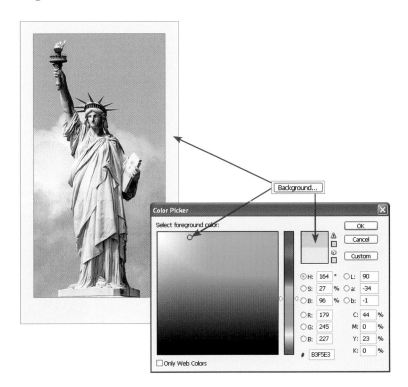

Matte

© John Slater

When images are professionally framed they often have a piece of card called a matte over the picture. Not only does this enhance the image, it also protects. Simulate a textured matte for a painting.

1 Open the file PaintingEND you made in Chapter 2. A version is also available on the Website.

2 Increase the Canvas size by twice the width of the matte required. In the example shown the dimensions have been increased by two inches to give a matte one inch wide per side.

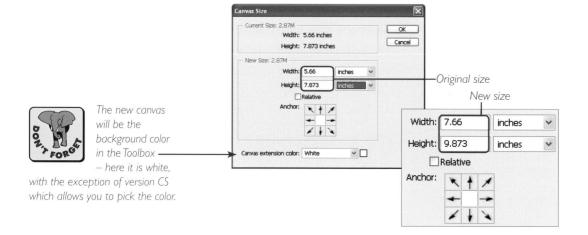

Original size

New size

The new canvas will be the background color in the Toolbox — here it is white, with the exception of version CS which allows you to pick the color.

3 Make a selection of the new canvas with the Magic Wand.

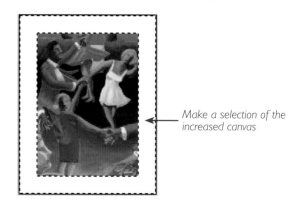

If you make the matte on a separate layer you can use it with other images.

Make a selection of the increased canvas

Use the Eyedropper to sample the painting for matching colors.

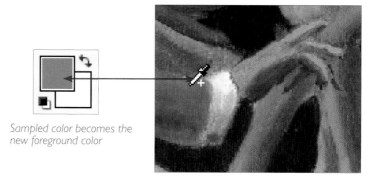

Sampled color becomes the new foreground color

4 Make a new layer, name it as shown, and fill (Edit > Fill > Foreground Color) with a color from the painting. You should end up with something constructed like the image below.

Usually a matte has more space at the bottom. If you want the matte to have unequal dimensions use the Canvas size box again.

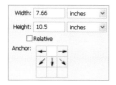

5 Add some texture to the matte to make it look like Ingres mounting board. Two steps are needed. First add noise using Filter > Noise > Add Noise.

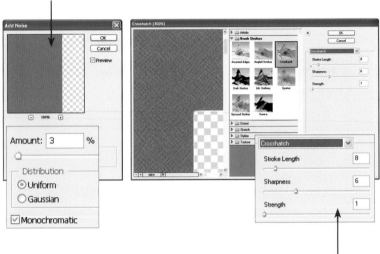

6 Then add a suitable filter. In the example above Filter > Brush Strokes > Crosshatch. Save the file.

Add a Keyline/Washline

High class framing often incorporates keylines or washlines on the mount. Here you will add a simple keyline to the mount just created. The task is made easier using a selection to position guides.

You may find this section easier to understand if you turn off the visibility of the painting layer (Background) when making the initial selection. The Gray Matte layer must be active.

1 Make a selection of the empty space inside the matte.

2 From the menu go Select > Modify > Expand. Choose 50 pixels.

When you expand the selection the corners are rounded – which you may or may not like. Use the Rectangular Marquee for square corners.

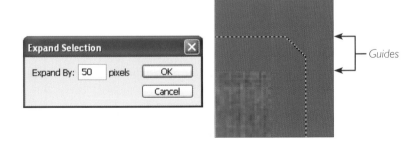

Guides

3 Drag guides to the edge of the selection.

Put the stroked selection on its own layer and keep the flexibility to bevel or emboss this line for even greater effect.

4 Use the Rectangular Marquee to make a selection inside the guides where the keyline is going to run.

5 Pick a suitable color, perhaps a light gray from the painting and Edit > Stroke. Set a suitable width (here 3 pixels) and click OK.

You may need to move the guides and deselect to see the Stroke.

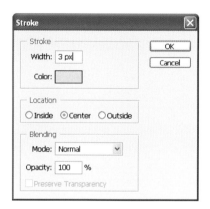

Finish with a Bevel

The finishing touch is a bevel — the tricky 45° miter so difficult in reality is a doddle in Photoshop.

1 Select the inside of the matte again and this time expand the selection by just 10 pixels.

2 Move the existing guides to this new position. Make additional guides along the edges of the painting. The area between the guides is where the bevels will appear.

3 With the Rectangular Marquee make a selection along the top edge of the image, between the guides.

4   To create the miter the selection needs to be modified. Pick the
    Polygonal Lasso and, whilst holding down the Alt/Option key, select
    the unwanted part as shown below. Fill this with a slight off-white color.

*In later versions of
Photoshop, buttons
in the Options bar
do the same trick
as the ALT key.*

*Move existing guides and add new
guides at the edge of the matte. Make a
selection of the area between the guides.*

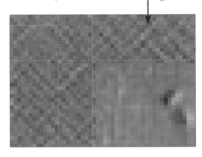

*Remove the area shown in
red and fill the rest of the
selection with white.*

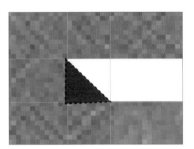

5   Repeat for the remaining three bevels, changing the color of each
    very slightly to create the illusion of depth.

6   Save the file as PaintmatEND.

Apply the Matte to other images

Once you have made a matte, on its own layer, it is easy to apply this to another image. You could build up a library of mattes if necessary.

1 Open the file Lion and PaintmatEND and arrange so that you can see both files.

2 Drag the Gray Matte *layer* from PaintmatEND onto the Lion using the Move Tool.

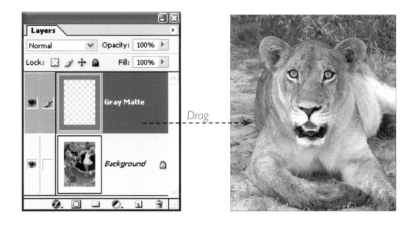

Drag

3 Adjust to fit using Edit > Free Transform. Simple really!

If you want to see all of the Lion picture increase the Canvas size first.

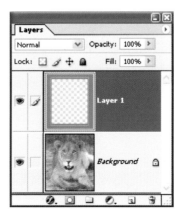

Framing

Will a wooden frame look better than metal? Now is your chance to try. With small frames it is easy, just scan them in and paste in the picture (see last section). You can also simulate sophisticated wooden and metal textures using filters applied in series.

Wooden frame

1 The picture below shows the type of wood you will "manufacture". Multiple steps are needed to achieve the effect and you can customize each one if you wish.

If you haven't already done so flatten the layers on PaintmatEND. A version of this file is on the website.

2 Open the recently completed file, PaintmatEND. Set the background color to white and increase the canvas by double the width of the frame required.

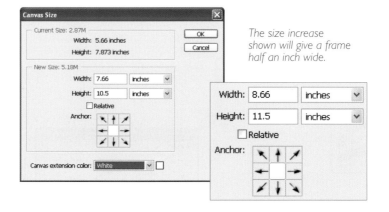

The size increase shown will give a frame half an inch wide.

3 Make a New layer and name it "Frame".

Click on the foreground or background color in the Toolbox to open the Color Picker.

4 Click on the foreground color to open the Color Picker and change the settings as shown next. Repeat for the background color.

Use the Tab key to move from one box to another.

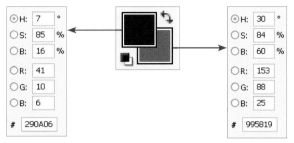

New foreground color   New background color

5 Apply the Clouds filter with Filter > Render > Clouds, and then add Noise using Filter > Noise > Add Noise.

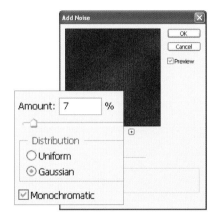

Don't be alarmed when your image is covered by black and brown – it is only the layer that is affected.

6 Follow this with Filter > Artistic > Dry Brush.

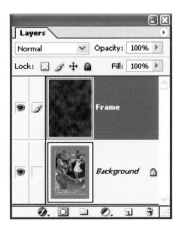

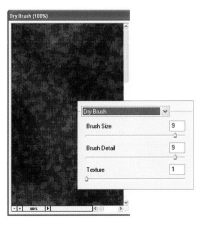

*Image >
Adjustments >
Contrast.*

7 Increase the contrast with Levels or Contrast dialog.

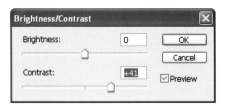

8 Apply the Shear filter using Filter > Distort > Shear. Adjust the line and watch the preview until you obtain something visibly pleasing.

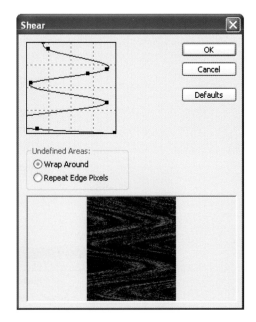

*Make sure this
box is not ticked
in the Options bar.*

9 Remove the center of the wood layer to make it look like a frame. Make a selection of the new white canvas on the *Background* layer. Swap the selection with Select > Inverse. Move to the Frame layer and press the delete or backspace key. You should now see a basic frame. Deselect and save.

*Layer Styles
were called
Layer Effects in
some versions of
Photoshop.*

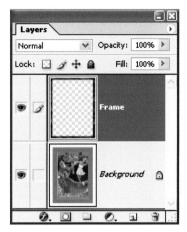

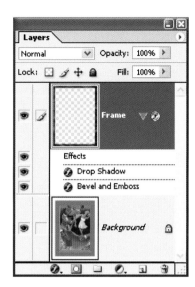

10   Add realism with Layer > Layer Style. Experiment with the many
     options. The example used the settings shown.

*Noise is used to
make other filters
more effective.*

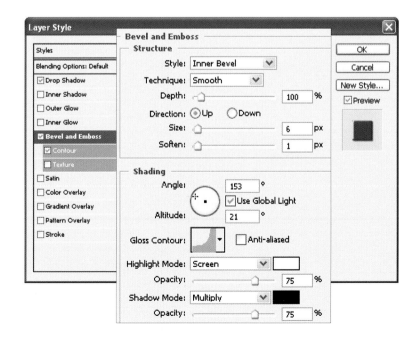

11   Flatten the image and save the file.

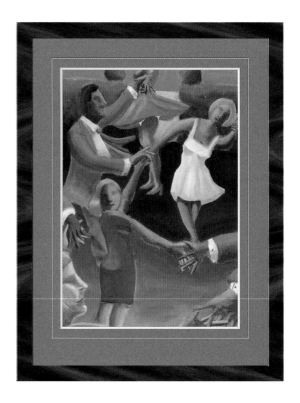

Subtle changes

Wood is notoriously variable in color. To alter the color and tone of the wood or to make it simply more funky use any of the adjustments you have come across in previous chapters.

In Photoshop CS, however, the Shadow/Highlight command offers most of the options needed. If available, try Image > Adjustments > Shadow/Highlights.

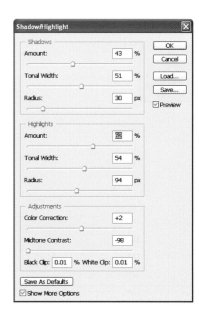

Frame Scam

Here you will put the image into the frame and adjust the image to fit. The frame size is fixed.

Image > Rotate Canvas > 90° CW.

1 Scan a small picture frame and your image. The examples shown here are the files Frame and Flower.

2 Make the Flower file active and from the menu go Select > All.
Follow with Edit > Copy.

3 Make a selection of the inside of the picture frame with either the Magic Wand or the Rectangular Marquee and Edit > Paste Into.

$+$

Even if you have many images open you can only work on one image at a time.
Make sure the active image (title bar highlighted) is the one you want.

4 The flowers appear inside the frame and on their own layer. Resize to fit with the Edit > Transform commands.

5 Flatten and save the file.

$=$

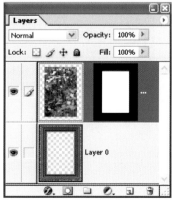

Big frame scam

© John Slater

With large images you have to re-size the frame to fit the image. A few unexpected problems arise and a few more questions posed.

1 Open the Frame file and the VolcanoEND panorama you made in Chapter 9. Drag the frame onto the picture.
They are totally dissimilar in size.

The completed panorama is available on the website.

2 Select and delete the inner white part of the frame. Make the frame fit using the Transform commands, but because the perspective of the two images is different it is inevitable that some distortion appears as shown below.

The frame is wider at the sides. Select these areas and delete.

Are you on the correct layer?

3 Solve this with some digital joinery. Select the two offending edges with the Rectangular Marquee and delete them using either the Delete or the Backspace key.

4 Use the Transform commands to stretch the cut sections of wood to the edges of the image.

If you do NOT want the image to be covered by the frame increase the Canvas size.

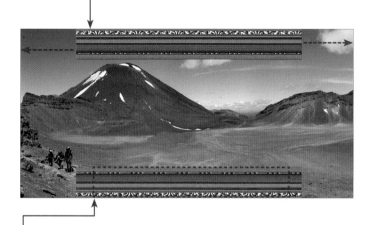

5 Select an area of the top moulding big enough for the sides – it doesn't matter if it's too big. Put this selection on its own layer with Layer > New > Layer via Copy.

6 Use the Transform commands to rotate the selection and move it to form one of the sides. All is fine except the new section is not mitered at 45°.

Hold down the Shift key as you rotate. This will keep the section perfectly upright.

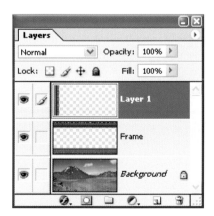

Rotate the selection into place, the areas of overlap will soon be cut away.

7 Pick the Polygonal Lasso and select an area of wood in the bottom right corner to "saw" away. Again delete.
Repeat for the top right corner.

Select the unwanted corner with the Polygon lasso.

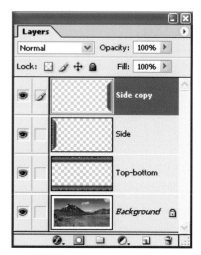

8 Rather than repeat the whole process for the other side – just duplicate the layer and reposition.

9 Merge the Frame sections (layers) into one and save the file.

Five Minute Wonders

To finish a few interesting effects and techniques – all are very quick – five minutes maybe stretching it a little!

Covers

Images used / created in these mini projects

Orion

Walker

BigBen

Heather

StepWedge

GrayshirtEND

Venice

Flowers

Chapter Fifteen

Make pencil drawings strong

© Sue Willmington

In traditional photography thin or poorly exposed negatives can be duplicated and then sandwiched together to increase their density and rescue the images. You will do the same thing in Photoshop to a whispy line drawing to make it more suitable for painting or adding textures.

1 Open the file GrayShirt.

2 Open the Layers palette and duplicate the Background layer.

3 Change the Blending mode to Multiply for instant results.

It may help to adjust Levels before duplicating.

4 Adjust the Opacity if the result is too strong or duplicate another layer if the results are still too weak.

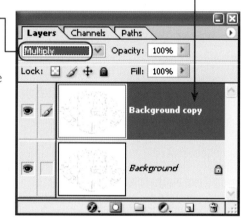

If the drawing is very light you may need to repeat the process to get acceptable results.

5 Flatten the layers and save the file.

Speedy Illustrations

© John Slater

It is surprisingly easy and effective to turn photographs into high quality illustrations. You may never want to draw again once you have experienced this powerful technique.

1   Open the file Flowers.

2   From the Menu bar pick Filter > Blur > Smart Blur.
    Experiment with the settings in the dialog box.

3   Click OK and save the file as FlowersEND.

Sending pictures by Email

There is an ever increasing demand for images to be sent over the internet as email attachments. Although Broadband is becoming more popular users still use relatively slow connections. It is important, therefore, to be aware of and control the size of the files you are sending.

Save layered files as PSD, flattened files as TIF and compressed files as JPEG.

Photoshop (*.PSD,*.PDD)
BMP (*.BMP,*.RLE,*.DIB)
CompuServe GIF (*.GIF)
Photoshop EPS (*.EPS)
Photoshop DCS 1.0 (*.EPS)
Photoshop DCS 2.0 (*.EPS)
JPEG (*.JPG,*.JPEG,*.JPE)
PCX (*.PCX)
Photoshop PDF (*.PDF,*.PDP)
Photoshop Raw (*.RAW)
PICT File (*.PCT,*.PICT)
Pixar (*.PXR)
PNG (*.PNG)
Scitex CT (*.SCT)
Targa (*.TGA,*.VDA,*.ICB,*.VST)
TIFF (*.TIF,*.TIFF)

1 Open any file and re-save, (File > Save As), but choose JPEG as the file format. Click the Save button and the JPEG Options dialog box will appear.

The higher the number the better the quality but the bigger the file

Compressed file size and download time

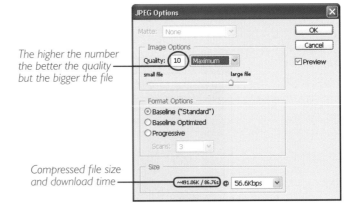

2 If the image is too big consider altering the Quality setting – the lower the quality the smaller the file.

3 If the file is still too big reduce the Image size and/or Resolution with Image > Image Size.

4 To send the file write an email and "attach" the image to the message.

The paperclip icon is a common shortcut for attaching files.

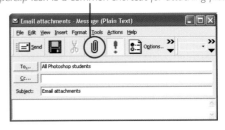

Make a Step Wedge

With some images it is good to include a known reference to allow easy color and tonal correction. A step wedge is the perfect reference. Make one to include with your digital files.

1 Make a new file with the dimensions shown below.

Reset colors to default black & white by clicking on this button.

2 Reset the color swatches in the Toolbox to the default pure black and pure white.

3 Drag a linear gradient from one edge to the other.

4 Create steps in the gradient with Image > Adjustments > Posterize. Use the setting shown below. Save the file.

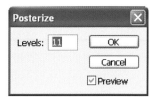

Patterns

© John Slater

You can easily turn any image or part of an image into a pattern. Test your results on a blank file.

1 Open any image and make a small selection with the Rectangular Marquee tool. If you want to follow the example shown here use the file BigBen.

2 Then Edit > Define Pattern. You will be asked to name the pattern, which is then stored in a library to be used at any time.

3 Make a new file – the dimensions below are suitable.

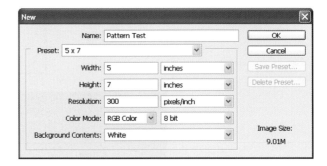

4 Edit > Fill > Pattern. In the dialog box set the options as shown below, and click OK. The blank file is filled with your pattern.

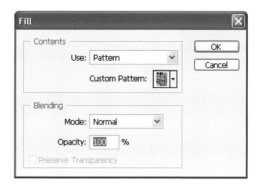

5 If necessary repeat the process defining different areas – some areas will work well others will not.

6 Calm the tiled appearance using Filters. Shown below is Filter > Extrude followed by Filter > Artistic > Fresco.

7 Save the versions you like.

Try making a pattern solely of text.

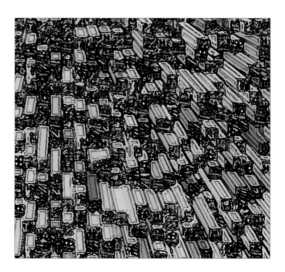

Chameleon – Color to B&W

© John Slater

There are many ways to change color to black and white. Two techniques are compared.

Desaturate

1 Open the file Orion and make a duplicate using Image > Duplicate. Save the files as OrionDESAT and OrionMIXER.

2 Arrange the files so that both can be seen on the monitor.

3 Turn the DESAT file into a grayscale image using Image > Adjustments > Desaturate, and save the file.

Mix it up

1 Make the MIXER file active and from the menu go Image > Adjustments > Channel Mixer.

2 Move the sliders around to get what you consider to be a good image. Hopefully you will make some improvements, but try and not lose too much detail around the face. Save the file.

Make sure the Monochrome button is ticked.

Sepia plus

© John Slater

Even easier than changing an image to black and white is changing it to a single color. Many old photographs are a sepia color, but you can make your images any color you like.

1   Open the file Heather and go Image > Adjustments > Hue / Saturation.

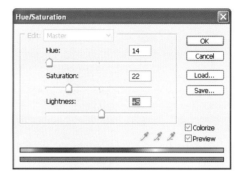

Make sure the Preview button is ticked.

2   Tick the Colorize button. The image goes a reddish-brown color.

3   Gently move the sliders around until you get a pleasant Sepia color.

4   Save the file as Sepia.tif, you need this for the next mini project.

It is easy to create monotone colored images with Colorize.

Vignette effects

© John Slater

Very popular in the early years of photography this romantic effect is easily recreated on the computer using selections.

1 Open the file Sepia you created in the last exercise (page 219).

2 Drag an oval selection with the Elliptical Marquee tool and soften the selection with Select > Feather.

If the selection is not as you want, move it or transform using Edit > Transform.

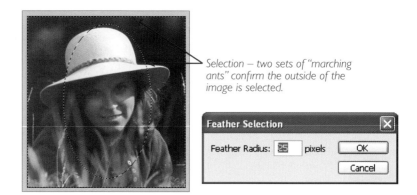

Selection – two sets of "marching ants" confirm the outside of the image is selected.

3 Inverse the selection with Select > Inverse.
You should see two sets of "marching ants".

The shortcut for a fill is Alt + backspace keys.

4 Fill with white or any color you choose. Save the file as HeatherEND.

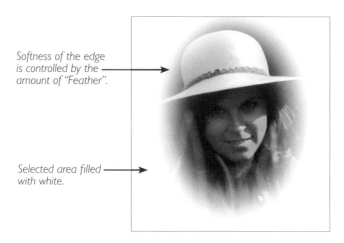

Softness of the edge is controlled by the amount of "Feather".

Selected area filled with white.

...cont'd

© John Slater

Darken the background

The same selection technique can be used to darken a background.

1 Open the file Venice and make an oval selection in the center of the image similar to that shown below.

2 Inverse the selection and feather.

3 Darken the selection using Levels or the Lightness slider in the Hue/Saturation dialog box. The effect is dramatic, and with the addition of some simple text you can easily transform your great photos into ever greater posters, cards etc...

4 Save the file as VeniceEND and close.

Image > Adjustments > Hue/Saturation.

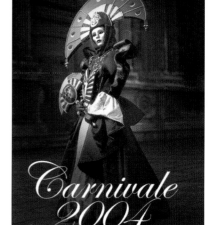

Family Tree

© Walker family

An increasing number of people are researching their family history. Here is a fun way to make the whole process more graphic. Plan your layout before you start this project.

1 Make a new file the same size as the paper in your printer – probably A4 or Letter size and give the page a pleasing color.

2 Pick the Rounded Rectangle Tool (in Custom Shapes) and set the Options as shown.

If your version of Photoshop does not have the Shape Tools use the Marquee Tools.

Moving objects is made easier if the Auto Select Layer is ticked in the Options Bar.

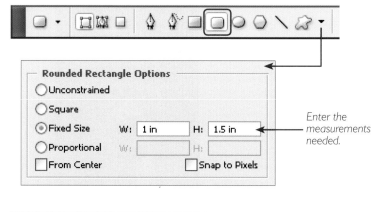

Enter the measurements needed.

3 Click on the colored page and a rectangle appears. Click any number of times to create more rectangles. Each rectangle appears on its own layer. Move the rectangles into position. These are the templates for your family photographs.

Check that this button is ticked in the Options bar.

4 Open the file Walker1 and Select > All, then Edit > Copy.

5 Make a selection of the appropriate rectangle with the Magic Wand and Edit > Paste Into. Adjust the position and size of the image within the box using the Transform commands. Discard the Shape layer just used – it has done its job.

Use grid lines for perfect alignment.

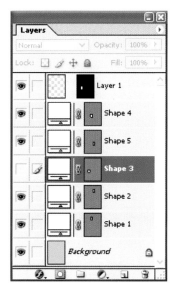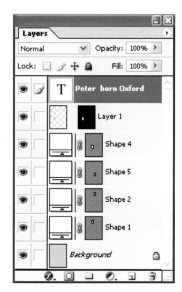

Color code different sides of the family with strokes, fills and glows.

Drag the layer you are working on to the top of the layer stack. Merge this with any associated type and then discard the shape layer.

6   Open the files Walker2, Walker3 and Walker4.
In turn Select > All, and Copy – Paste, into their respective rectangles. Very quickly you will build up the family tree.

The rectangles will be the foreground color. If this is the same color as your page nothing will be visible.

7   In the Layers palette turn off the visibility or delete the shape layers that have been used.

8   With the Type Tool add descriptive text beneath each Rectangle. Position the text above its associated photo in the Layers palette and join the two layers by Merging Down. Now the image and text are as one.

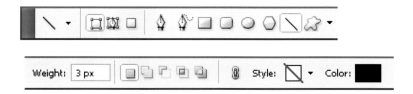

...cont'd

Each shape appears on its own layer. If you have a version of Photoshop that does not have the Shapes Tools, use the Rectangular Marquee to make the boxes and the Pencil Tool to draw the lines.

Hold down the Shift key to keep lines straight – or even better use guides.

9   Pick the line tool and draw lines, again noting that each line appears on its own layer. Merge layers to keep the palette simple.

10   When all is complete flatten the image and save the file. Hopefully you will be encouraged to try this with your own images.

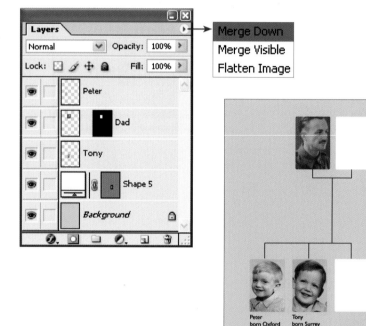

Instead of the Rectangle you might like to use other shapes – a few examples are shown here. Remember you can paste into these shapes as well.

Understanding Color Management

As you become more skilled in Photoshop you will inevitably become more demanding. Typically you want the colors you see on your monitor to resemble what you see in your prints. This last project shows how to set up your computer and what the strange messages mean when you open some files.

Covers

Images to use in this final project

Trulli

Inthepink

DSC_1183

Chapter Sixteen

Let's play tag

Color management attempts to control colors from the creation stage through to the final print. This is not easy because each piece of imaging hardware interprets color in a different way. To assist the workflow each device is tagged to indicate how it perceives colors. The tag is known as a color profile. This profile is attached to an image file and "translated" by the next device used. This continues until the image is printed. Tagging is the key – but all images are not tagged and some have tags you might not like – so how do you proceed?

Basic steps in a color managed workflow

1   Calibrate your monitor.

2   Set up Photoshop for color management.

3   Edit the image.

4   Control the output of the printer.

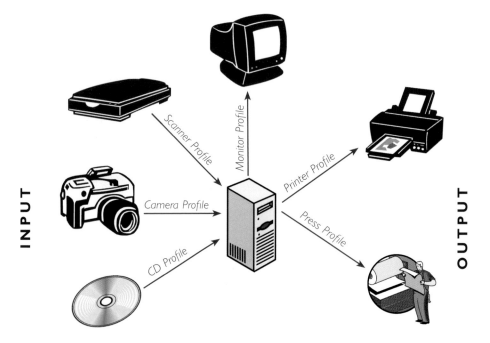

Calibrate

The first step is always to calibrate your monitor. Do this at frequent intervals. The best way is to use a piece of hardware from manufacturers such as Pantone or Gretag. Failing this you will have to get by using software included with your computer. This is typically Adobe Gamma or Display Calibrator. Even if you don't do this now the rest of the chapter will still be valid – but do it soon! Here you are guided through the process:

1 The process is reasonably straightforward. Just follow the instructions on the screen. You may need the instruction book for your monitor to confirm how to use some of the controls. On the Mac go to System Preferences and choose Displays. Pick the display profile for your monitor and press the Calibrate button.

Use a white point of 6500°K.

2 In Windows the usual place to find Adobe Gamma is Start > Settings > Control Panel > Adobe Gamma.

Not all screens are shown.

Introduction screen

A series of screens help you adjust contrast, brightness and color

Choose 1.8 Gamma for the Mac and 2.2 for the PC

The suggested white point is 6500°K

Give the new profile a specific name

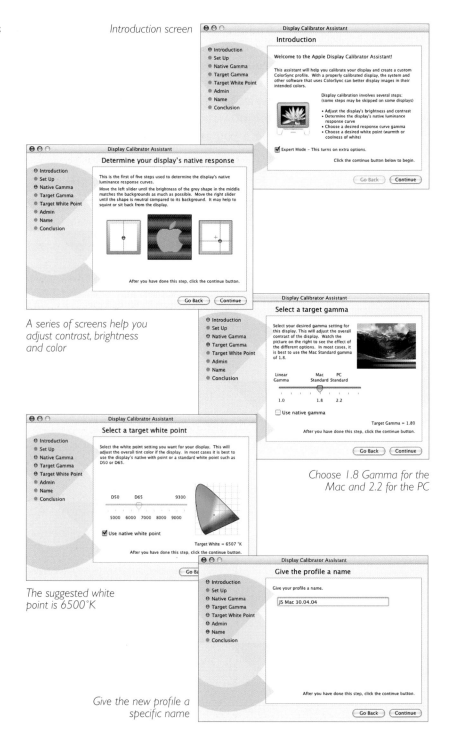

Color Settings

In the Color Settings dialog box, you can choose from a list of predefined color management settings or adjust the controls manually to create your own custom settings. You can even save customized settings to share them with other users and other Adobe applications that support color management.

1　Go to the Color Settings dialog box. With Mac 10.3 and Photoshop CS follow Photoshop > Color Settings. With Windows XP and Photoshop CS follow Edit > Color Settings. Other combinations of Photoshop and operating system will be similar.

2　Use the settings shown unless you have a good reason not to.

3　Save the settings with an obvious name.

Adobe 1998 is suggested for most users and sRGB for web designers.

Set a Gamma of 1.8 for Macs and 2.2 for PCs.

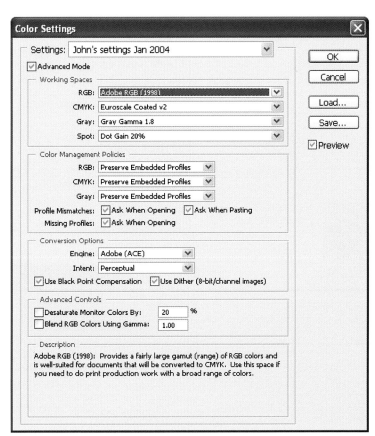

Working profile already assigned

© John Slater

The easiest form of color management is to have your images tagged with the working profile – all then happens transparently.

1 Ensure that your color settings are as shown on page 229 and open the file Inthepink.

2 Nothing visible should happen – the file should just open. It is already tagged with the Adobe 1998 profile, the suggested workspace setup earlier.

3 If, for some reason, you wanted to change the tagged profile you have two options from the Image > Mode command.

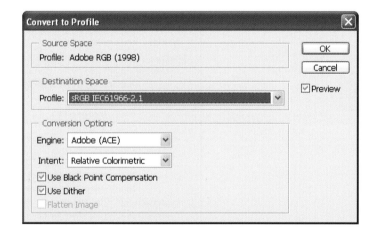

Don't change a profile unless you are sure you know what you are doing!

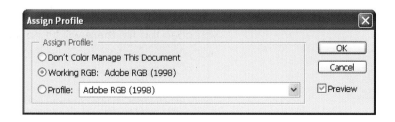

No profile assigned

© John Slater

All medium to high end scanners and digital cameras now offer the ability to tag images with a profile. Some do not, plus you may have lots of old scans etc that are not tagged. These are referred to as legacy images.

1. Open the file Trulli and you will be confronted with the following dialog box.

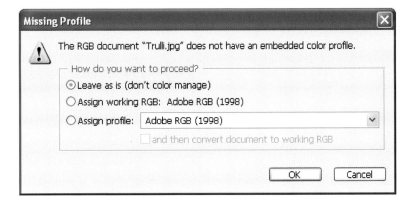

2. Generally you will assign the working profile you set on page 229. You may, however, like to look at what happens when you choose a different profile.

3. If you assign the working profile as shown above, the next time you open this file there will be no message. The image will have the working profile embedded.

sRGB profile already assigned

© John Slater

Is this a color space to be careful with? This demonstration will not work unless your color settings are as shown on page 229. You are going to see changes a different profile makes. Only you can choose which you prefer. With many scanners and digital cameras the sRGB profile is automatically assigned.

Open the file DSC_1183 or any of your photographs which have an sRGB tag. If you are using the Adobe 1998 color space you would probably change the assigned tag here, but in this case keep the sRGB embedded tag.

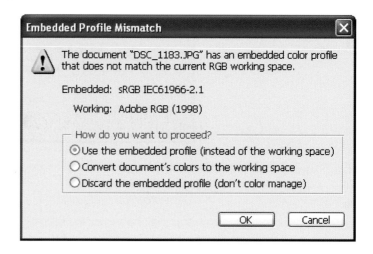

 For some strange reason files may be saved with an sRGB tag even though this was not requested. In these cases choose "Discard profile" when opening and embed Adobe 1998 when saving.

Duplicate the image and save without a tag (untick the box in the save dialog box). Save the duplicate as a TIF and close this file.

Open the new TIF file and assign the Adobe 1998 tag. View the two images side by side and observe the differences.

The proof is in the print

Don't think that just because you have done all this technical stuff you are going to get in print exactly what you see on the screen – because you will not. The best you should hope for is a fair representation and something you are pleased with, and something more consistent and predictable than an unmanaged workflow. There are two options:

Print with Preview is the same as Print Options in v6.

1. Let Photoshop do the color management.
2. Let the printer do the color management.

It is important to choose one or the other and not both.

Printing controlled by Photoshop

Set up color management so that either Photoshop is in control OR the printer – NOT both.

1 Open any file. The one shown here is Flowers.

2 Go File > Print with Preview and select the settings required, specifically the kind of paper you are printing on.

Check Page Setup for correct printer, paper size and paper orientation.

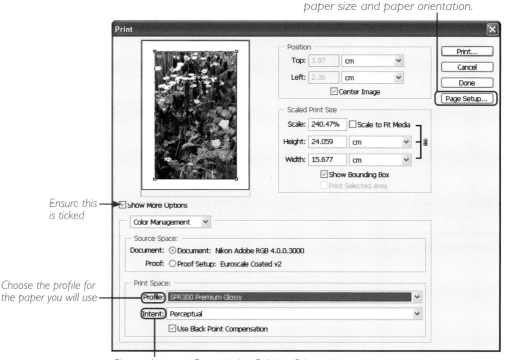

Ensure this is ticked

Choose the profile for the paper you will use

Choose the intent. Perceptual or Relative Colometric should be the choices for most users.

3 Confirm required settings, specifically turn the printer color management OFF.

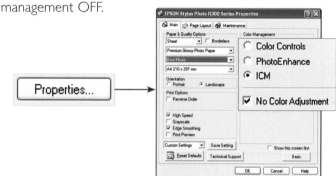

Printing controlled by the printer

Open any file, the one shown here is DSC_1183. Again go File > Print with Preview and in the Print Space choose "Printer Color Management".

If you print this image you will need to change the orientation to Landscape in Page Setup.

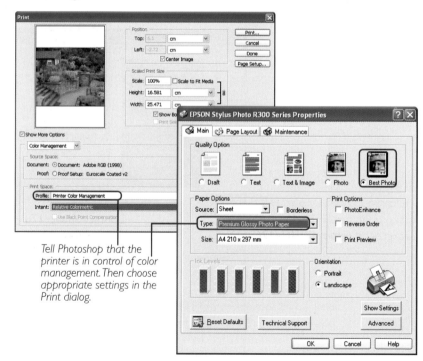

Tell Photoshop that the printer is in control of color management. Then choose appropriate settings in the Print dialog.

2 Choose "Print" and adjust printer settings as required.

Index